THIS IS HOW IT WAS

THIS IS HOW IT WAS, so many years ago that horses shied when a gas buggy snorted by; when it was unadulterated bliss to ride on an open trolley and as adulterated terror for a little boy to squeak a few halting words "long distance" to the county seat four miles away.

This is how it was when a penny bought candy "fried eggs" in a tiny tin pan, a big soft pretzel, a sugared waffle hot off the griddle, or a block of ice cream. When the Fourth of July meant firecrackers and a big parade and Decoration Day meant honoring the dead. When movies cost a nickel and the Sunday School picnic was free. When the Old Reliable was better than the New Improved. When the butcher, the baker, the farmer, and the umbrella man came to the door and the doctor came to the patient.

This is how it was when God *was* in his heaven and all *was* right with the world.

THIS IS
HOW IT WAS

Illustrated by   *Sylvia Gilman*

by William J. Laubenstein

DILLON/LIEDERBACH, INC.
Cleveland
1971

S. Gilman

THIS IS HOW IT WAS
William J. Laubenstein
1971

Published in serial in THE WEEKENDER,
Oct. 3, 1970—Jan. 30, 1971,
The Pottsville *Republican,*
Pottsville, Pennsylvania.

Published in book form by
Dillon / Liederbach, Inc.
14591 Madison Avenue,
Cleveland (Lakewood), Ohio 44107.

TO MY FATHER
A kindly, honest man

S. Gilman

Looking Over My Backyard Fence

This Was Our Town

Teddy Roosevelt had settled the great Anthracite Mine strike of 1902. The eight hour day was here to stay. Deep-throated colliery whistles called men to work six days a week, eight hours a day. From the flatlands between the West Branch of the Schuylkill River and Wolf Creek, the town was spreading up the slopes of the seven hills that surrounded it. Our main street stretched a mile from the Philadelphia & Reading depot to "top of town." It was sloppy in spring, dusty in summer, and ice-hard and rutty in winter. Stores had awnings that gave shade in summer and shelter from rain and snow.

North was Mine Hill Mountain, split by Mine Hill Gap. Still further north was the massive Broad Mountain, separating the two great anthracite coal basins of eastern Pennsylvania. South loomed the knife-like bulk of Sharp Mountain. Beyond was Pennsylvania Dutch country—fertile farms, sturdy bank barns, stone houses. The land of hex signs, quaint old-country customs, strange but delicious foods.

Our town was a polyglot—Pennsy Dutch, Polish, Greek, Russian, Hungarian, Irish, Welsh, Italian, Lithuanian—a dozen more. Each day immigrants, tagged like so much freight, trudged to Mike Boruch's general store and steamship agency. The men walked stolidly ahead, old country caps firmly on head. The women trailed dutifully behind, shouldering tiny trunks that held their most precious possessions. They were herded to the nearest mining patch where cheap labor was needed in the mines. Another American family was born.

There were three schools—one a high school—many

churches, stores of all kinds, dozens of saloons. Gold was more plentiful than greenbacks. No one bought on "tick"— credit. Luxuries came dear and were paid for in cash. There were no chain stores.

The houses were honestly built for honest living. They were mostly of wood and stood on the narrowest of lots, wall against wall, porches jutting out on the sidewalks. Few of the lots were more than 25 feet wide. Land was scarce. The Company wouldn't sell—or if it did, sold grudgingly. The Company, of course, was the Philadelphia & Reading Coal & Iron Company. The Company owned our town, the land about it, the woods on the hills, the laurel in the thickets, the coal under our homes.

Some of the houses had electric lights. Our town had its own electric light plant. Most of the houses had only coal oil. Heat was by coal stoves. Coal was cheap. There was one street for the well-to-do. That was called Quality Hill. All the houses on the Hill had electric lights. Some even had telephones. Banker Steel had the most imposing house on the Hill. It had pillars, just like homes in the South.

The railroad linked our town with the rest of the world. The railroad was the Mine Hill & Schuylkill Haven and it was a part of the Philadelphia & Reading system. There were eight connecting trains for Philadelphia each day. Our big city newspapers came from Philadelphia by early morning "paper" train—*North American, Inquirer, Ledger.* No one ever heard of the New York *Times.* Electric cars took us in to the county seat, four miles away, for a nickel.

Of an evening, young couples seriously courting walked from the depot to "Top-o'-Town" and, if the boy had a little money to squander, stopped at Geanslen's for ice cream.

Babies were born, children grew up and went to school. Most quit at 14 when they could get their "papers" and went to work in the breakers or in the shirt factory or knitting mills. Some, a very few, went on to High School and fewer still went to Normal Schools to become teachers, or to college to learn the law or medicine. People went to church, married, begot children and were taken care of in their old age by their children. And they died, were decently mourned, and were buried in family plots.

It was all unhurried and unharried.

Fannie and Jonas

The year Fannie and Jonas fell in love, Fannie's father was planning to move his family to Brooklyn, New York, within a few months. This move would be another momentous one in William Harris' life. He hoped and prayed that this time he would have more luck than in the past. Twice before his great decisions had brought him nothing but trouble and near-bankruptcy. He and his wife, who was Adeline Wythes, had taken their small children by steam train and by stagecoach to the oil fields of Western Pennsylvania, there to drill for fortune. On the way their trunk, with all their possessions, had fallen from the boot on the rear of the stagecoach, and they arrived in Clarion, Pa., with only the clothes on their backs. With the little money he had, he hired a drilling rig and tried his luck. Two dry holes brought him to the sad realization that he was broke. (That the wells "came in" a year later when another driller went fifty feet deeper was small solace.) So William Harris and his family came back to the hard coal regions, where he had spent his boyhood and young manhood.

There he secured a lease on some anthracite coal lands, erected a tipple from native timber, drove a drift into the side of Pine Hill mountain and began to take out coal. The vein showed promise, and at last it seemed as if prosperity was beckoning. Then, one black night, the tipple caught fire and collapsed. His workmen, given a choice between taking their pay or waiting for a month until repairs were made, chose money. Again Lady Luck deserted him. (Years later the same lease sold for more than a million dollars.)

Now opportunity loomed again. William Harris had secured the post of superintendent of the Lithogranite

Manufacturing Company in Brooklyn. The firm made "artificial stone, side walks, horse blocks, chimney tops, coping, sewer and well pipe" in the new age of concrete. In December, 1885, William Harris left, alone, for the big city. His wife and children were to follow him by summer. Fannie didn't want to make the move. She was in love with her Jonas and eager to make her home in Minersville. She urged Jonas to write her father for her hand.

Jonas wrote, and this is the letter he received from Fannie's father:

Brooklyn, New York, Jan 12th, 1886

My dear young friend:

Yours dated 10th inst came to hand, and I have carefully noted the contents. Having entire confidence in you and Fannie, I have not the slightest objection to her becoming your wife. I am sure she will prove a good and faithful partner to you as her mother has to me. You are both no doubt aware that you are about to assume a very great responsibility. You must both look well into your own hearts and determine whether you are prepared to relinquish all selfish desires for each others good. You must live for and have full confidence in each other to be entirely happy. If either one does anything that displeases the other you must never allow your angry passions to arise, but treat all such matters in a spirit of love and kindness. If you do so I am sure you will live happily together. It is my sincere desire that you will do so. I am pleased to learn that your parents approve of your choice, as it speaks well for Fannie. I hope and feel confident that she never will prove unworthy of their confidence. Wish-

ing you a long, prosperous and happy life together, I remain
sincerely your friend

                              Wm. H. Harris.

On June 17, 1886, Fannie and Jonas were married in the
front parlor of the Harris' brick house on North street. William Harris came on from Brooklyn to give his daughter
away. A few weeks later the Harris family moved to the city,
and Fannie and Jonas set about living their own lives
together.

In 1896, I arrived to have, in time, the little adventures
that are told in the pages following.

Christmastime

This is how it was, at Christmastime.

After the chestnuts had been gathered, the walnuts shucked, the hickory nuts laid by for the winter, after the prayers of thanks for the bounties of God at Thanksgiving Day, it was time to think of Christmas.

The days were chill. Maybe there was a powdering of snow, but nothing much. Ice skimmed the ponds and promised skating soon to come. On a bright Sunday afternoon, after Sunday School and church and dinner, my father said to my mother: "Fannie, get the big basket, it's time to gather moss for the Christmas tree!"

We walked miles and miles and miles, or so it seemed to a lad going on six, (actually it might have been a mile) to woods that had not yet felt the destroying axe. In the darkest, scary parts, when the sun shown dimly, we found the bright green moss growing rank in the black, peaty soil. I dug in the spongy earth trying to lift big pieces of the moss in my little fingers. When I had one dug, it joined the growing heap in the basket. Some of the moss was almost black-green. Some was lighter. After the basket was filled, we sat down in the silent woods. A red squirrel jumped nervously from limb to limb on a pine tree. My father could talk to squirrels. He'd "Chrr . . . chrr . . . chrrrr" at the red squirrel, and the squirrel would answer "Chrr . . . chrr . . . chrrrr" back. I wanted to know what he said, but my father just said, "Some day I'll tell you . . . not now." Back home mother took the moss down into the cool cellar and laid it out on the floor for keeping until Christmas.

Then, one day, father came home with a triumphant grin. "Fannie," he said importantly, "I got the company perMIT

today." That's the way he pronounced it, and I have ever since.

This was big news. It meant that the "Company"—a great monster akin to those pictured in my fairy-tale books—had told father he could cut a Christmas tree on "Company" property. And it must be remembered that the "Company" —the Philadelphia & Reading Coal and Iron Company— owned just about every acre around our town.

Other years I had been too little. "Next year," father would say when I begged to go with him.

But this WAS next year!

Now father's idea of a Christmas Tree was perhaps not in the best traditions of woodsmanship. We went out in the woods, and he looked and looked. And I looked too, not quite knowing what I was looking for. Then, suddenly, he stopped and said: "That one, William. That's the tree for us!"

But the tree he picked out was terribly tall—almost as tall as our house, or so it looked to me. I just knew it would never, never fit in our house. But father laid at the ten-inch-thick trunk of the hemlock, and soon it was stretched out. Then, expertly, he lopped off the TOP of the tree. Then I saw what he had seen—a perfect Christmas Tree. (Of course there was a deal of waste in this method; but nobody seemed to care.)

We carried the tree home (I toted the very tippy end of it). Father whistled while we walked. It was a Christmas tune! "Tannenbaum." We put the tree on the back porch, there to stand for the admiration of all until the eve of THE DAY.

Santa Claus would trim it, of course. But I was allowed to help set up the big wooden quarter circle, corner fitting, six-inch high base in the parlor. There was a hole in the middle of the base, and that was where the tree fit into a pan of water beneath. After father had put the tree in place and stayed it with wires, I was allowed to put the moss in place to make a green carpet. There, I knew, Santa would put a mirror for a pond, with goldfish and ducks, and a little village with people and houses.

There were so many wonderful things a small boy wanted: a Flexible Flyer sled, a pair of ice skates, some marbles (glassies or aggies, of course, though I knew in my heart that the big boys would annex them as soon as mud showed through the snow), a Magic Lantern (you could give shows with that optical marvel which, lighted by a kerosene lamp, would throw colored pictures on a white sheet), Richter's stone blocks (with which you could build real houses and churches and barns). You wrote a letter to Santa Claus for the one thing you wanted most. And you hung your stocking. So too did father and mother. (You were always so sorry when mother got only a few candies and father got an onion, while your own black-ribbed cotton stocking was stuffed with candy and nuts and a big navel orange.)

Sleep finally did come Christmas Eve. But it fled around five o'clock in the dark of a wintry morning when father called upstairs and said: "Santa's been here!"

Racing downstairs in your nightgown you stopped open-mouthed. The Tree had been transformed into a wondrous tower of glitter and light. There were all kinds of ornaments, most of them from Germany. At the very top was a tinsel Angel. Real candles, perched in holders with heavy lead weights to keep them upright, shed a warm glow that unlocked the aroma of the hemlock.

This year that I was going on six I had asked for a Flexible Flyer sled. But it wasn't there. My lips quivered.

I think father had a tiny smile on his face. I'm not sure. What I remember was that he reached into the big pocket of his smoking jacket and pulled out—a real live puppy!

The white puppy was a nondescript fox terrier with one brown eye and a corresponding brown ear. He was tense and wriggling all at once as I held his warm, fat little body in my

hands. And I said: "I'll call him Gyp!" not knowing whether it was a him or a her (it was a him).

I put him down on the carpet, and he yipped happily and ran round and round and then stopped suddenly and made a puddle on the carpet. I started to cry because I was sure Gyp would be taken away from me. But mother just took a rag, mopped up the puddle and said: "Merry Christmas, William!" And my father said: "Merry Christmas, William!" —and Gyp wiggled so hard that he said it too.

The Flexible Flyer? Oh, Santa had been so excited over delivering Gyp that he forgot to bring it in the house. I found it on the back porch.

Shooting in the 20th Century

How much of this I truly remember and how much I remember because it was told to me I can't say. I was only three, going on four. At any rate, here is how the Twentieth Century arrived in our town.

At ten minutes to twelve on New Year's Eve, 1899, my father took his big gold Hamilton railroad watch from his vest pocket and placed it on the dining room table. That watch always kept perfect time as long as he lived. Regularly each month Jeweler Gerz checked and adjusted it to a split second. We knew it would tell exactly when the Twentieth Century arrived. He put his .32 calibre nickel-plated revolver beside the watch. Near the side porch door, he placed his 12-gauge double-barrel shotgun.

My mother dressed me warmly in blue reefer coat, leggings, scarf, mittens, and wool cap. She gave me an old tin dishpan and a big stirring spoon.

The three of us sat at the table as the seconds ticked away.

When the old year had but three minutes to run, my father pulled on his overcoat and hat, took the revolver and the shotgun and stepped out on the porch. I followed him with my noisemakers. Mother bundled up in a thick woolen shawl. It was crisp, clear, starlit; and there was utter silence. I didn't know what was going to happen. Maybe the New Century would start yowling or thundering or like that. My father looked at his watch in the glow of the light through the window.

"Ready, William!" he said, softly.

I held the spoon over the pan.

From the Town Clock on the Second Street schoolhouse came the first stroke of 12.

13

"Happy New Year! Happy Twentieth Century!" my
father shouted. As fast as automatic fire came five shots
from his revolver, sparks from the black powder cartridges
blazing like roman candles in the dark. "Bang! Bang!"
roared the shotgun.

"Happy New Year," I yelled, beating furiously on my tin
pan.

From our neighbors came the echoing shouts of "Happy
New Year! Happy Twentieth Century!" From all over our
town came the noise of horns, dynamite explosions, gunfire,
bells, whistles. Every colliery watchman held down his whistle cord in the engine rooms—Lytle, Pine Knot, Oak Hill,
New Mines, Phoenix, Glendower, Thomaston, Johnny
Davises. Every church bell pealed. The shirt factory, our
factory and the knitting mill whistles joined the din. The
engineer on a coalie heading up mountain with a string of
empties yanked at his whistle cord and clanged the big
locomotive bell.

In all the churches people gathered for Watch Night ser-
vices. As the bells rang and the whistles tooted, worshippers
prayed for their dead of the dying year and prayed for God's
guidance in the brand new century just born.

The old century was dead. The new century had been
properly "shot in." The church crowds came out into the
brisk winter air. We went back in the house, and mother
made us some hot cocoa to warm us up. I was pretty excited
even if I hadn't *seen* the Twentieth Century, whatever it was.

On Fourth of July eve, we always thought the noise of
dynamite explosions would bring rain. Maybe the racket
on New Year's Eve brought snow. At any rate, about this
time of year in our town, snow began coming down in earnest.
The roads were worn ice-smooth, sleighbells replaced the
clopping of hooves. On every hill sleds flashed, loaded with
shouting kids.

Today snow is a nuisance, except in the ski country. It is

something to be fought with shovels and scrapers and bulldozers, with salt and chemicals that melt, but kill. It is
something to be cursed.

But to us, snow meant coasting, bobsledding, and sleighride parties.

In our town, snow came lazily in December, piled up a bit
by Christmas, came in great storms in early January, abated
a bit in the annual "January Thaw," then buried us anew in
late January, February, and into early March. We took the
snow as it came, we didn't fight it. The more snow came
down, the better the roads. Even the horses liked the snow,
for sleighs are easier to pull than wagons. And as for us
kids. . . . .

Snow is the reason why I still owe the estate of Adam
Hinkel, blacksmith, the sum of eight cents. At interest the
way the First National Bank used to pay—one per cent per
annum—this debt would not loom too large at this late date,
even if the interest had been compounded. However, that
eight cents is still a debt on my conscience.

Snow meant a bob-sled, this particular winter. My best
friend "Scow" Zapf and I pooled our resources and came up
with a cheesecutter each—one badly the worse for wear and
age; a plank about ten feet long and a foot wide—this from
the yard of the Zapf brewery on Sunbury street; some odds
and ends of scantling and such like scrap wood, some rope,
and most important, ten cents. Our project seeming well
financed, we got things under way.

Our greatest need was hardware—specifically some nuts
and bolts to put our bobsled together. "Scow" and I hustled
over to Adam Hinkel's blacksmith shop to strike a bargain.

The blacksmith shop in summer was cool and shadowy
dark. But in the winter it was a chilly cave, black dark,
lighted only by the coals that glowed redly in the forge and
turned white-hot when the bellows roared air under them.
The huge bellows was worked by a handcrank which turned

a set of wondrous gears that raised and lowered the bellows.

"Scow" and I were in no hurry to buy our nuts and bolts, for Mr. Hinkel was putting winter calked shoes on a big draft horse. Three were already on. This was an interesting project, and we stood by to see that it was done properly. "Scow" and I took turns cranking the bellows' mechanism. The coals got white-hot. Mr. Hinkel heated an iron shoe and pounded it to his liking on the big anvil. He plunged it, hissing, into the barrel of iron flake-specked, dirty water alongside the anvil. He tried it against the nigh (near) front hoof. Critically he gauged what corrections should be made. We cranked the bellows. The shoe was reheated, hammered, cooled, tried again. It looked like a good fit to us experts. Now he reheated the shoe, and cooling it slightly, applied it to the hoof. There was a hiss and a stench of burning horn.

We winced in imagined pain, though we knew there was no more feeling in the hoof then there was in our own toenails. The shoe fitted perfectly. In went the horseshoe nails, to be crimped so they would not work loose. The horse shivered a bit as he stood gingerly on the calked shoes, then shook his head impatiently that he was ready to go.

Mr. Hinkel turned to us. *"Was wollen sie, knaben?"* he asked, as if we were his most important customers.

Well, we boys wanted four three-inch bolts with washers and nuts, and one five-inch bolt with four washers and two nuts. He reached a grimy hand in the big bins along one side of the dark shop and handed us the hardware. *"Wie viel?"* we asked. Mr. Hinkel took a stub of a pencil and figured on a bit of board.

Eighteen cents! Our bobsled budget was shot full of holes. It was out of balance. There was a deficit. It was something akin to budgets, high and low, today.

Ah, we recalled, after our first shock, there was always "tick."

Easy budget payments, borrowing to pay vacations, to buy

a TV set, borrowing to pay for the expected baby was something far, far in the future. In our town there *was* credit available, but no one in his right mind would buy on "tick." "Tick" was a dirty word.

Having admitted that this was undoubtedly so—in our joint and childish minds—we proceeded to buy on "tick."

We proffered our ten cents, our entire capital, to Mr. Hinkel. He took it in his black hands as if it were gold. We promised the big blacksmith under our most solemn oath that we would come back right away with the eight cents balance—surely tomorrow at the very latest—if he would only trust us. *"Ja! Ja! Ja!"* he nodded sourly and doubtingly. We ran happily away.

We never went back. Other pressing matters engaged our attention. We just plain forgot our debt. Which is the reason why I still owe the estate of Adam Hinkel eight cents, coin of the realm.

Happily back in my yard, the building of the bobsled began. We used the four smaller bolts to attach the worn cheesecutter to the plank at what was to be the stern of our craft. Now a cheesecutter was a sled that was rapidly giving way to the Flexible Flyer. The Flexie was by all odds the greatest sled ever developed—and still is. But the cheesecutter had its points. For one thing, it was low-slung—perhaps five inches high from iron strap runners to the wooden deck. The runners curved in front, and the iron straps ran the length of the runner and up to the top of the curve. There were two handholds, one on either side, right back of the curved runners. These were to grasp when you ran with the sled, flopped bellybumpers and skimmed down the hill. A cheesecutter was a good fast sled for all purposes, but lacked the steering qualities of the Flexie. You used a boot-toe for a brake and body English to steer.

On the better cheesecutter we screwed a reinforcing piece of wood six inches wide and an inch thick across the deck, about in the middle. We put another piece of wood about four inches wide at the very tip of the ten-foot long plank. Now we bored a hole through this reinforced end down through the reinforcing piece on the cutter and dropped the five inch bolt through, putting a washer under the bolt head on top, two between the cutter and the plank, and one under the nut at the bottom of the bolt. The second nut was a "jam nut" to keep the other one tight. That gave us steering easement between plank and cutter. We screwed a piece of wood about two inches wide and three feet long on the protruding deck of the cutter for steering. Ropes were attached to the ends of the bar for hauling, and our bobsled was ready. She could take around ten kids if they scrunched together.

We tried her out on our street, then took her over to Quality Hill where the run was about a half mile from top of the hill to Sunbury Street. She was fast, even before we slicked the runners by rubbing them over coal ashes.

We took her out almost every evening after supper, when the weather was good. We made the run from the top of the hill to Sunbury Street in about three minutes if we had a full load aboard. Some of the people who lived at the top of the hill used to ride down with us when they were going to the stores at night, especially on Saturday night. We had to watch out when we crossed the branch line tracks on Railroad Street. There wasn't much traffic at night, but sometimes there would be a coalie from the Stoddard Washery. Then we had to ditch the sled.

The run down Bullshead Road was longer—a short mile —but more dangerous. The run was almost straight, and when you reached the main line of the railroad, you were really tearing. We always had a "flagman" there to warn us to swerve off the road into the freight yards if a big coalie was coming down the mountain or an empty going up.

I never took our sled on Kelly's Hill. That was more than a mile, with corkscrew turns, steep, sharp grades, and a run

right across Sunbury Street traffic near the end. My father said NO to this hill. He was right. It had a history of broken bones.

Longest and fastest bobsled run in the county was up Ashland way. I made it once with my cousins when we were there on a visit. We hitched the sled on to a horsedrawn pung bound for Centralia at the top of Centralia Mountain. We walked beside it. The run was almost four miles from the top of the mountain down to Center Street in Ashland, with a sharp left turn onto Center and a fast run the full length of the town, adding another mile. If riders were able to make two runs in an afternoon or night, they were lucky, but it was worth it.

Collier Kear was our organizer for sleighride parties. We called him "Lad." None of us knew, of course, that years later he would save the lives of countless young boys around the mines. He developed a means of cleaning slate out of anthracite coal so that breaker boys were no longer needed any more and there no longer was that terrible cloud of coal dust hovering over the breaker—the coal dust that ringed breaker boys' eyes in black and filled their lungs with the black dust that would bring "miners' asthma" or silicosis.

Lad charged us fifty cents for the sleighride and fifty cents more for a fried oyster supper in Schuylkill Haven, where most of our sleighride parties landed. When I was a seven-year-old, I went on a sleighride for the first time, but we only went to Pottsville. Schuylkill Haven was twice the distance—about eight miles.

Fred Zimmerman, livery stable proprietor, got Lad's business. He had the best sleigh. It was about twenty feet long, with seats all along the sides. The floor was covered with straw to keep your feet warm. When he had a full load of kids, Fred used two horses. We were constantly under snowball fire as we trundled through the mining patches and the little farm towns. Retaliation took some time and sometimes meant a fast run for the sleigh, for the driver never stopped for these skirmishes.

We got a half dozen big fried oysters, fried potatoes, bread and butter, cole slaw, a hunk of pie, and a glass of milk or a mug of cocoa for our half dollar. The driver got his fried oysters free as a sort of tip. Of course he didn't drink cocoa. The fact is, by the time we started back the driver would haul himself up on the driver's seat, pull a buffalo robe about him, head the horses home, and fall fast asleep. The horses didn't need directions or the whip. They knew the sooner they made the stable, the sooner they'd get some hay and oats.

We skated on all the little ponds and ice dams, but our pride was what we called "The Park." This was a square pond scooped out of the clay by mine mules and scoop shovels. In the summer it was populated by small catfish, smaller sunnies, and a multitude of small fishermen. In the winter time the Fromm boys cleared off the ice and opened The Park for business. They charged a nickel for the use of the shanty to put on your skates around an old woodburner stove there and you could come in to warm up. A coal oil flare atop a pole gave night illumination.

Winter was the season for wars and rumors of wars. Snowball fights raged from the first snow to first mud. Our Carbon Streeters could take the measure of the Quality Hillers (they were sort of sissy-like), but when a challenge came from the Newcastle Street gang, it was time to make a truce with the Hillers, enlist them, however soft, on our Carbon Street side and prepare ammunition.

Snowballs came in regular, soakers, icies, and just plain messy. Soakers were the ideal ammunition as the snow began to melt and snowballs could be soaked in the runlets of icy water before using. Icies were soakers left out overnight to freeze. These were lethal weapons—and I mean it. The messiest of snowballs were those made in early spring when snow, mud, and road gravel, with an occasional bit of horsedroppings, went into the making. Besides being messy, they left their target an equal mess.

Our wars never came to a real conclusion. The ringing of the school bell or the cries of various mothers herding their kids home brought armed truce.

That was our winter when snow was a friend to be cherished by man and beast and not battled with sand, salt, bulldozers, chemicals, curses.

My Father Could Powwow

My father could powwow.

He was not a *hexadukt'r*—an evil one who could *verhex* people and cast spells on them and do them hurt. My father was a good man, and he could help cure people. He didn't call himself a doctor. He never took money for the good things he did to people. That would have been wrong. It would be like taking money from some one because you said *Gesundheit* or "God be with you."

Mrs. Fenstermacher was one who believed with all her big Pennsy Dutch heart that he had "the powers." He was a seventh son, and that was enough for her.

Mrs. Fenstermacher was a huge woman. Nowadays a doctor would have taken one quick look at her and run for the diet tables. Mrs. Fenstermacher liked her vittles, as did most Pennsy Dutch. She liked to eat her chicken and waffles, swimming in good rich gravy, with a big mound of mashed potatoes. And she adored sauerbraten and *sauerkraut und speck*.

I always knew when Mrs. Fenstermacher would come to our house. And I knew why she came. She wanted my father to powwow the big growth on the side of her neck. It was fiery looking and it was so big that it swelled out over her dress and she had to fix the collar of her dress so she could get it around her neck. She always wore a long scarf, winter or summer, wrapped around her swollen neck. Even when she went to church she kept the evil thing covered up. I used to look at it in church and it sort of made me sick to my stomach to see it.

Mrs. Fenstermacher always came to our house just before the moon was full. That was what my father told her. She would knock on the side porch door and my mother would let her in.

"Good evening, Mrs. Fenstermacher," my mother would say.

"*Guten Abend,* Missus," Mrs. Fenstermacher would reply. She didn't speak English *sehr gut* so she said most everything in Pennsy Dutch. Pennsy Dutch is a mishmash of English and German. Most all the people in our town spoke it. But my mother was stubborn Welsh and she wouldn't even say *Wie gehts.*

Mrs. Fenstermacher would say "Is your man Yonie to home, please, missus?"

My mother would call "Jonas!" and my father would come out and shake hands with Mrs. Fenstermacher.

"*Wie gehts,* Mrs. Fenstermacher," my father would say. "*Wie gehts bei Dich?*"

How was it going by Mrs. Fenstermacher?

Mrs. Fenstermacher would take off her scarf. From the far reaches of the kitchen I would peek at the evil growth.

"*Ist besser, nicht wahr?*"

My father would nod judiciously. "*Ja,* it looks better."

"Will you do it again, the powwow, please, Yonie?"

"Do you believe, Mrs. Fenstermacher?"

"*Ach, Ja, Ja,* I believe!"

And the fervent tone of her "yes, yes" was evidence that she indeed believed that God in his infinite mercy could cure all the ills of the world—if all believed in Him.

They would go out on the side porch and my father would put his right hand on the swelling. The moon was shining serenely down through a cloudless sky. He would say, softly, to his patient: "Look, Mrs. Fenstermacher, look now on the moon and tell God you believe." Then he would stroke the growth and say, in Pennsy Dutch, "Now what I look at increase! Now what I stroke decrease! In the Name of the Father, and of the Son, and of the Holy Ghost!"

S. gilman

He would repeat this three times. Mrs. Fenstermacher
would wrap the scarf around her neck again. She would say
a fervent *"Danke, danke schoen"* and my father would
gravely accept her thanks as an accolade. She would take a
little worn purse out of her pocket and would offer my father
money. But he would never take it. "The Son of Man took
no money for his good deeds. Neither should man take from
neighbor just for a good deed," he would say and then:
"Good evening, Mrs. Fenstermacher, come back when you
see the moon coming on full again."

A dozen years later I was at Mrs. Fenstermacher's funeral
with my mother and father. The undertaker may have done a
good job, but look as hard as I could I couldn't see much

swelling in her neck. My mother said: "Well, Jonas, you have lost a good patient." "Well," my father said, "I don't think I lost a patient. Doc Kistler may lose them. Any rate, I don't think I ever killed any patients of mine. Doc Kistler can't say that."

Powwowing is pure faith healing. When I was small there were powwow doctors in every rural community. Like my father, they were kind, simple, religious men—men who believed implicitly that God could heal. Powwowing is an act of prayer, an act of appeal to God Almighty to exert his powers to cure. No one need be ordained to pray. Every man can pray. The Bible tells us in countless passages that faith and faith alone can cure. Every powwow incantation—and there are hundreds of them—ends with the exhortation "In the Name of the Father, and of the Son, and of the Holy Ghost."

Of course many of those who believe in powwowing are superstitious too. But aren't we all? Don't we dodge on the other side of the street to avoid walking under a ladder? Don't we shudder at breaking a mirror? Don't we knock on wood to ward off evil? Don't we shun black cats?

But powwowing is more than superstition. It is an act of simple faith. It is a belief that God can heal if our faith is strong enough. That is the secret of the powwow doctor.

There were two women in our town who could powwow. One we called "Aunt Minnie" Beach. The other was affectionately known as "Auntie" Sarah Bright.

Aunt Minnie actually lived for her powwowing. She had a record of cures. She could take out "the fire" for certain. That was erysipelas—that burning and itching of the skin that was so much more common years ago. She carried a skein of bright red woolen yarn with her. She would take a bit of the red yarn and draw it across the inflamed parts and she would adjure the fire to leave the body, always in the name of the Father, Son and Holy Ghost.

"Auntie" Bright used this incantation for the same disease:

> "Wildfire and the dragon flew over a wagon,
> The Wildfire abated and the dragon skated,
> In the name of the Father, and of the Son, and of the
> Holy Ghost."

"Auntie" Bright could cure warts. Maybe we were an unstable bunch of kids in those days because most of us had warts. Nowadays dermatologists attribute warts to nerves. Be that as it may, we used to go to "Auntie" Bright and try to show her our warts. She would peer at our outstretched hands and say: "Go home. Wash your dirty hands. How do you expect me to see warts in that filth?" When we came back she would look at the warts and she would rub them and rub them. Her fingers were soft and it was sort of nice. Then she would say something in Pennsy Dutch that I couldn't understand. But she would say at the end: *"Im Namen des Vaters und des Sohnes und des Heiligen Geistes."*

And the warts DID go away. Was it faith?

"Aunt Minnie" would be called for all sorts of ailments. If someone had a bad inflammation she would take a clean rag and wet it with cool water. She would lightly bathe the inflamed part and make three crosses with her thumb. Then she would say: "Sanctus Itorius res, call the rest. Here the Mother of God came to his assistance, reaching out her snowwhite hand against the hot and cold brand. In the Name of the Father, and of the Son, and of the Holy Ghost."

She would repeat the three crosses and the incantation three times, waiting about two hours between the first and the second spells and coming back next day for the third time. The inflammation *would* vanish. Was it faith?

If you had a bad bump on the head and it really hurt, you would run to "Auntie" Bright's house and she would rub the lump and say:

"Bruise, thou shalt not heat. Bruise, thou shalt not sweat. Bruise, thou shalt not run, no more than Virgin Mary shall bring forth another son. In the Name of the Father and of the Son and of the Holy Ghost."

The pain *did* go away. I know. Was it faith?

"Aunt Minnie" and "Auntie" Bright each treasured a tattered copy of the workbook of the powwow doctor, the famous *"Lange Verborgene Freund"*—"The Long Lost Friend" by John George Hohman, first printed in America in 1820. In this book were countless spells, recipes, magic symbols, prayers for good and to ward off evil. If you carried the book around with you, the author declared, you were "safe from all enemies, visible or invisible; and whoever has this book with him cannot die without the holy corpse of Jesus Christ, nor drown in any water, nor burn up in any fire, nor can any unjust sentence be passed upon him. So help me." And in his preface to the book he says: "Is it not written expressly in the 50th Psalm, according to Luther's translation: Call upon me in the day of trouble, I will deliver thee and thou shalt glorify me." And Hohman adds: "All this is done by the Lord."

In evil opposition to the powwow doctor was the *hexa-dukt'r* or hex doctor. He was a sorcerer. He could verhex a person. He could cast spells. He could turn milk sour, cause cows to go dry, cause beef cattle to die, grain to rot, crops to fail, people to fall sick and die. The powwow doctor dealt in simple faith. The hex doctor dealt in the spells of witchcraft.

Not in my childhood, but many years later—in 1929— eastern Pennsylvania was stirred by the famous hex murder trial of three men in York. They were accused of killing one Nelson Reymeyer, a man they said had cast a spell upon one of them. A hex doctor had told them that the only way to break the spell was to take Reymeyer's copy of "The Long Lost Friend" and to secure a lock of his hair. They were to dig a hole eight feet deep and bury the hair in it. In the process of striving to break the spell, Reymeyer was savagely beaten and died of the effects of the blows. His death seemed to mean nothing to the three, especially to the one who had instigated the assault. After he had been convicted, he welcomed the penitentiary sentence with: "Now I can sleep and rest and eat again. The hex is gone from me."

My father believed in the hex. But he believed that faith in God could overcome the evils of the hex.

This was a story he told me about a hex. He said it was a true story because it happened to one of his cousins down in the Long Run valley, out from Cressona. This is the story:

"That fall I went hunting squirrels down on my cousin's farm. He had a big farm, maybe a hundred acres of fine land, with a big bank barn, a tight old stone house, a big corn crib and all kinds of outbuildings. He had horses and cows and chickens and he raised pigs for winter meat and to sell.

"When I got to the farm—I took the train to Beck's Crossing—he was a cousin of mine, Dave Beck was, and we talked about the family that was scattered around the valley. Pretty soon my cousin John came by in a spring wagon and we started out for his farm. He was always a pretty lively man, about my age, and always had a lot to say and lots of farm kind of stories to tell that were good for laughs. But this time he was mighty strange and quiet.

"We drove for a couple miles and he finally just quit what talking he had been doing. Maybe another mile and I couldn't keep from asking: 'What's wrong, John? You ain't like you used to be.'

" 'Jonas,' he said, shaking his head. 'My farm is *verhexed!*'

" 'Come now, John,' I said, 'You don't believe in a hex nowadays do you?'

"He nodded his head solemnly. 'Believe it or not, may farm

is *verhexed.'* Then he talked more and more excitedly. 'My best cow has run dry. My old hunting dog Jeff got caught in a bob-wire fence and got so bad cut I had to shoot him. I didn't get half a crop o' corn this year and what there is of it is half filled out ears. You know my well that gives such good water. That ain't run low for long as I can remember. My father dug it almost in Indian time. Well there's mebbe a foot or so of water in it right this minute. I got to haul water for my stock. No one else has to do that. Everybody got water but me. And my chickens got something wrong with them. They're droopy and I ain't getting many eggs. I tell you, Jonas, my place is hexed.'

"He sat there, limply holding the reins, shaking his head.

"I said to him, 'John, I gotta agree with you that sounds like someone put a spell on you. What are you going to do about it?'

" 'Well, Jonas, I know as how you powwow. I thought. . . . .'

" 'Whoa, John,' I said, 'I never had anything to do with breaking spells. Oh, I can do some powwowing, but *hexa-dukt'rin'* ain't in my line.'

" 'Yep, I know. Sorry I asked, Jonas,'

"Well, I stayed with John and his family for three days. And, believe it or not, I didn't get but one gray squirrel all that time. John said the hex was working on them too. I had to believe it.

"I didn't hear anything from John for a couple months. Then, about Christmas time I got a letter from him, written in Pennsy Dutch and sort of hard to make out. Writing Pennsy Dutch and talking it are two different things. No two Pennsy Dutchmen will write a word the same. It's all sort of phonetic, as you know. Well, John was a happy man, according to his letter. The hex had been broken. Everything was going fine on the farm. Then he told me how it happened. He went to a hex doctor and told him his woes. The hex doctor wanted to know who might have put the hex on him. John said the only thing he remembered was that he and his neighbor Ike Nunemacher had had a fight over a line fence and Nunemacher threatened to go to court about it. 'Ah, hah!' the hex doctor said, 'That must be it. But that hex must be right in something on your farm. Are there any stray animals around?' John told him that a black cat was prowling around the barn but wasn't bothering anyone, just catching field mice. 'That's your hex,' the hex doctor said triumphantly. 'Now to get rid of it. You take a silver dollar and melt it down and make a bullet out of it. Then put the bullet in your shotgun and shoot that black cat dead. Then dig a hole six feet deep and put that cat in the hole head down. Put a forked stick over the cat to keep it that way and then fill up the hole. Then say 'In the name of the Father and of the Son and of the Holy Ghost' three times and turn around three times, each time ending up facing to the east.'

"John wrote that he did just as the *hexadukt'r* said and the hex vanished. Everything was good again on the farm. There were lots of squirrels in the woods, eating the late nuts and if I came down next year I'd be sure to have sport. And he was right, I never had such good hunting before or since. That hex doctor knew what he was doing."

When my father died, years later, I found a worn copy of John George Hohman's "Long Lost Friend" in his writing desk. In it I found a paper and on it he had written a charm again all evil:

"The peace of our Lord Jesus Christ be with me. Oh, shot, stand still! in the name of the mighty prophets Agtion and Alias, and do not kill me! Oh shot, stop short! I conjure you by heaven and earth, and by the Last Judgement, that you do no harm unto me, a child of God. In the Name of the Father, and of the Son, and of the Holy Ghost."

He believed.

Paris Comes to our Town

Medicine, or whatever passed for it, came to our town in varying forms. If it hadn't we never would have seen a genuine Paris gown.

Our town had what might be called a split personality— and split in several different ways. For one, it lay just on the southern border of what was in those times the immense Pennsylvania anthracite coal fields. Yet, not too far to the south there were farms which grew in productiveness as the barrens and culm banks of the coal lands gave way to the red shales of Pennsy Dutch Berks County.

The people of our town were split too. There were the old time families and, lumped all together, the immigrants who came over to work in the mines, to save their money and, in another generation, become Americans.

Our town slept during the week. There was little store trade. The small knitting mill hummed sleepily. The miner trains pulled out at five thirty in the morning for the Heckshersville Valley, dropping off miners and laborers at Oak Hill, Mine Hill Gap, Pine Knot, Thomaston, Glendower, and for New Mines, Silver Creek, Phoenix Park. The trains would return around six at night, to dump off tired, coal-black men whose sole thought was getting most of the grime off their faces and hands, eating a solid meal and falling into bed.

But on Saturday night our town came alive. Saturday was pay day in the mines. And the pay was in good hard money, not greenbacks. Before I knew what a silver dollar looked like I knew the double eagles ($20), eagles ($10), and five dollar gold pieces. The immigrant didn't like paper money. He had seen his bundles of rubles and lira or zlotys dwindle

31

at Ellis Island Immigrant Station to a small fistful of "American." But silver and gold—that was money.

So, with good hard money in their gnarled hands, smiles of honest expectation on faces pitted with the blue specks of coal driven into pores by the force of black powder or dynamite blasts, they descended on the town from nearby mining patches, bringing their wives with them. The women bought in the stores. Their men zeroed in on their favorite saloons.

Our town had a record that made the clergy wince, that made the drinker laugh, that made the temperance White Ribboners despair. The bald facts were that our town had 7200 population—and 76 saloons.

And on Saturday night all the saloons were jammed. Most of them vied with each other with inducements like "Kid Roast Tonight," "Sauerkraut and Pigs Knuckles" or "Free Lunch." A "kid", of course, was the gamey offspring of the almost wild goats that roamed refuse banks at the coal mines, eking a spartan living from the wiry grass that grew in the coal dirt and—we were sure—from the coal dirt itself. "Free Lunch" could mean anything from a bowl of beer pretzels—rock hard and saltier than the ocean—to sliced meat, sausage, potato salad, cheese, crackers. All that was required to partake of the bounty was the price of beer— five cents for an eight-ounce schooner, ten cents for a big sixteen-ounce growler.

As the gold coins clinked on the mahogany bar, the beer flowed in floods. Giant muscles flexed, faces waxed wroth, sweat beads stood out, fights were common. This was expected. Fights that started in the saloons were quickly transferred to the streets when the battlers were summarily thrown out the swinging doors. But fighting only built up a new thirst and soon all was forgiven and the foes made up over another schooner of cool beer.

The Dutchmen—the farmers who, with their wives and

kids, had come in for groceries and a beer or so—had their own grocery and general store run by one Johnny Klein, a simple, jolly Santa-Claus-belly of a man whose proud boast was that he could down a hundred oysters in a stew and who held the town beer drinking championship of 31 schooners in a single evening.

The Dutchmen congregated at Schultz's saloon up the street from Johnny Klein's store and there quietly drank beer until their wives picked them up, poured them into farm wagons and headed the tired horses homeward. At which point husband, wife and kids all fell asleep and let the horse find his own way. Which he invariably did—having visions of oats and hay ahead.

Saturday night, of course, was one night when we children didn't have to be in the house by sundown. We could stay "over town" until ten o'clock that night. There were the fights to be seen. There was candy to be bought, if you had saved your pennies during the week. There was ice cream too, but a little dish was expensive at a whole nickel. There were "things" to be bought at Will Jones Stationery Store —maybe a nickel "Rocket" baseball (which was only slightly better than our own gumball-wrapped-in-store-string kind), jacks (that was girl stuff), a baseball bat (at a whole quarter, this was for the rich), rubber balls on an elastic that you could bounce on the pavement and it bounced right back at you, crayons (for a nickel you got at least a dozen of all colors). Then there were the nickel novels—Pluck and Luck, the Liberty Boys of '76, Old and Young King Brady, Arietta and Young Wild West. These were like money in the bank, once bought. For you swopped your copy to some other lad, who in turned swopped it to someone else and then you swopped the one you had got by swop and sooner or later someone was stuck with a bundle of tattered paper, almost unreadable. But that original nickel sure worked for us.

But I've gotten away off from the genuine Paris Gown.

Well—on almost every street corner on Saturday night there were pitchmen peddling all kinds of gadgets and guaranteed sure-to-cure medicines, salves, pills, liniments. Over packing case counters kerosene flares lighted the wares. We spent most of Saturday night listening to the pitchmen's spiels, wishing we had the money to buy the wonderful jackknife with the half dozen blades, corkscrew, pry, gimlet, file packed into its magic innards. We knew the blades would bend—except for the sample one the pitchman was using to demonstrate. . . . . but. . . .

Kings of the corners were those showmen who sold such things as Snake Oil or Swamp Root. One had a real live Indian in a feather war bonnet and a tomahawk who did a war dance right there in the street. He pounded his feet into the dust and gave warwhoops and then took a big swallow of the Swamp Root to show that that was what made him strong. My father said he drank so much they had to put him in the lock-up to sleep it off. I wouldn't know about that.

But one week these little side shows paled. Down on the flat, near the railroad bridge over Wolf Creek, a real showman set up in business. He sold Beaver Oil, which was guaranteed to take the stiffness out of a marble statue—he had a statue too. This Beaver Oil man not only had coal oil flares, he had dozens of them. He had a big tent back of his platform and there were runways going out from the platform into the crowd. From the tent minstrels came out, all in blackface and they played banjos and cracked real funny jokes. And then there was a girl came out in a real short dress and she sang songs while a man in a funny looking suit with long tails to his coat played a violin. It was pretty nice music. Sort of sweet. And then there was a funny band that played jewsharps and mouthorgans and sweet potatoes and horns and a big drum. Then there was not one, but six real Indians that did "tribal" dances—that's what the Beaver Oil man called them. And in between each act that Beaver Oil man sold his stuff at a dollar a bottle—six for five dollars. The way he talked even I wished I had a dollar, even if my muscles didn't need limbering up and I had no rheumatiz.

Well, I'll tell you, the saloons might just as well have shut up that night. The storekeepers yawned over their "tick" books. Will Jones didn't sell a nickel novel.

Everybody was down there watching this big free show. The miners and their wives and the Dutchmen and their wives and all the kids cheered every act. And that Beaver Oil man had to get some of his Indians to help him bring out bottles he was selling them so fast. When the selling got slow he'd run on the platform and say there was another big act coming.

And sure enough there was.

All the time he was bringing on those big acts he kept telling us there was going to be a gigantic great big surprise finallee just before the performance ended for the evening. He wouldn't say what it was but everyone stayed there and waited and waited and bought more Beaver Oil. Well, it got awful late and all us kids were afraid it would be ten o'clock too soon and we would have to go home or get a licking. But we couldn't have gone away even if we wanted to. We were sort of glued to the spot to see this great big mammoth surprise.

And then it came almost ten o'clock and the Beaver Oil man came out with a brandnew white leather outfit on, with a stiff shirt and a big diamond stickpin. The coat had long tails and he had white shoes on. He came right out front and said: "Laaadies an' gennelmen, you have been most patient tonight. You have been the greatest audience my performers have ever appeared before. And they have appeared before the crowned heads of Europe and the great moguls of Asia. You have gratified me by buying that most miraculous liniment that I have offered for sale—Beaver Oil. I thank you, and we all thank you for your attention. And now, the gigantic, colossal surprise that I have been promising you all evening." He stopped for a moment. Then he said: "Laaadies an' gennelmen, right before your very eyes I wish to present to you my gorgeous wife . . ." he stopped again "wearing her genuine evening gown from Paris, France."

Then this woman stepped out on the stage and she was wearing a great big feathered hat and a dress that sparkled all over as she trotted up and down the stage, and we kids just went home.

Some surprise!

When We Called the Doctor

I never saw what was inside the green cloth bag Doc Kistler brought the babies in. That there were babies in it, I never doubted. But how big they were, what colors, whether they could holler and cry while they were in the bag, I never did find out.

I did know what Doc Kistler carried in his regular black bag—the one he carried when he came to our house because somebody was sick.

You called the doctor as a last resort. There were plenty of home remedies around for most any ailment known to man. And, of course, you could be pow-wowed.

Laudanum drops were for a teething baby, for an aching tooth, for an ill-defined pain anywhere. There was opium in laudanum; you could become a dope fiend from it. Sometimes when we saw a little baby that didn't cry a lot, we thought he was doped. There was sweet oil—that was to put in an aching ear. And flaxseed—if you got something in your eye, mother would drop a tiny, shining brown flaxseed under the upper lid. Then you screwed your eye up tight and most often the flaxseed would pick up the dirt and bring it down to the corner of your eye. If your eye was swollen, your mother would put cold wet tea leaves in a white linen cloth and bind it around your eye.

There was fennel and pennyroyal and boneset—all of them made various teas good for fevers or ague or some such. Pokeberry juice cured palsy and jaundice—we called it yellow janders. For rheumatism, a bath of warm salt water was good. A poultice of mustard, mixed with horseradish, garlic, and vinegar put on as hot as the patient could stand it was very good. My grandma, when she was old and lived

S. gilman

with us, used to put Sloan's liniment ("Good for Man or Beast") on her aching joints. Then she would drink a half glass of gin in which some garlic cloves had been steeped. Maybe it didn't cure her arthritis, but she outlived my dad—she passed away at the age of 94.

Cobwebs stopped minor bleeding. A moist cud of finecut tobacco, pressed against a wound, did a miracle healing job.

Of course there *were* germs. We heard about them. There were even pictures of them, all hairy and with legs and arms and teeth, in the Sunday *Inquirer* funny pages. But we didn't worry too much about them. The nicotine in the tobacco probably took care of them, and maybe we were so tough that the dust in the cobwebs carried only mild little germs that couldn't fight back. Besides, we wore asafetida bags around our necks. The dictionary says asafetida is "the fetid gum of various Oriental plants." It was fetid all right. No germ could stand the stink.

Sassafras tea was a spring tonic. My "Auntie" Bright used to stew the roots up and it was pretty good. Now Fellows Compound Syrup of Hypophosphites was rotten nasty. It was sort of light green and came in a biggish bottle. I had to take some every night because I was puny. My father took it too. He wasn't puny. I never tasted anything worse. We never had sulphur and molasses. I guess maybe it wasn't tough enough for our town in the hard coal regions.

Castor oil! I can taste it still. The taste is downright horrible. But worse than castor oil was kerosene and sugar. This was supposed to ease a sore throat. The sugar was sort of a "treat" to make the kerosene go down. We called kerosene "coil oil," which was coal town language for coal oil. As for the sore throat, you couldn't feel the soreness for the horrid taste of the oil, which, I suppose, was the cure. I heard one time that Doc Kistler used a feather wet with coal oil to break the white throat film in a diptheria case. I don't know whether it did any good, but Doc Kistler was always trying.

My mother used to send me over to Mrs. Reed's for some cramp medicine. Mrs. Reed was an old woman whose mother was one of the first settlers in our town. She had been noted for powwowing and for her skill in treating burns and dressing them. My Mrs. Reed concocted her medicine of herbs she had gathered in the woods. She had the "receipt" from her mother. It cost 25 cents a bottle. Probably it was some sort of Lydia Pinkham stuff. It was good, though. I tasted some once.

Headache powders were made up by Druggist Clemens while you waited. They were done up in little paper packets and cost a penny each. Sweet spirits of nitre was the universal fever remedy.

But the trouble with many of these remedies was that sometimes they didn't work. Then it was time to "CALL THE DOCTOR."

This was a serious moment. First, if you were going to call the doctor, the house must be "red up." If the place was a mess, the doctor might tell his wife what a slob you were. Doc Kistler's wife was not noted for her reticence. She could, and did, gossip over the fence as much as her neighbors. And the patient had to be yanked out of bed, washed, and decked in a fresh nightgown, then put back in a fresh-linen bed.

Calling the doctor could be done in one of three ways. You could dispatch a child, at the going rate of a penny, with a note asking the doctor to come. You could run down to the Lytle Store and call him on the telephone. Or, in nighttime emergency, father could hurry up to Doc Kistler's home on Quality Hill, wake the exhausted gentleman by pounding on the door, and alert him to the situation.

Doc Kistler was what we called, "Dutchy." He talked a sort of English with a Dutchy lisp. You always took his medicine "wis" a little "vasser." "Zis" was a fair translation of "this." And so on.

When Doc Kistler arrived, he would take complete, utter charge. The family gathered around the bedside and held their breath, literally, to hear the verdict. He was a big man, with heavy, almost black, hair, a full beard that he had brought back from Antietam and Gettysburg, and the softest of hands. His eyes were sad, as if he had seen too much of a suffering world. He was quiet, gentle, and confident. He had studied medicine under good old Dr. Beach.

He would feel your pulse and look at your tongue, using the handle of a clean spoon as a tongue depressor. He would feel your forehead for fever and ask a few patient questions. Then, diagnosis made, open came the black bag, exposing a fascinating display of colored pills in rows and rows of bottles. Doc Kistler was a homeopath. The dictionary says that homeopathy holds that disease is cured by remedies which produce in a healthy person effects similar to the symptoms of the complaint of the patient. There was another breed of doctors called "allopaths," but we didn't know what they were and cared less. Father would most certainly not have trusted one of them inside the front gate.

Doc Kistler would measure out some sugar pills in a little bottle, pour a few drops of bitter liquid over them, and present them to mother. She would be told to "gebt sem wis a little vasser" every hour or so. Or maybe he would give some of the colored pills. Sometimes he would ask for a glass of water, add the drops to it, ask for a little glass plate to cover it, and direct the giving of a spoon each hour or so.

Don't think I underrate Doc Kistler's ability. He was that rare person—almost extinct in modern days—the family doctor. The family's problems were his personal problems. If his remedies didn't work, he was the first one to dip into the past and try some oldtimer.

Like an onion poultice.

Now poultices were many and varied. They could be mustard, or bread and milk, for instance. A poultice was used to "draw the fire" out of an infection, either visible or inside. A bread and milk poultice was made by making a paste of a bit of soft bread without the crust and some hot milk. The paste was put on a piece of linen rag—old linen napkins were hoarded for this purpose—and the whole bound round the infected part. This was particularly good for evil-looking, yellow-green infected fingers. We called them "felons." One of the virtues of this was that after the poultice had dried as hard as rock, which it soon did, you could pull it off to see how things were progressing and shock the little girls at school.

The onion poultice was something else again.

This concoction was the nightmare of the devil in one of his most satanic moments.

It was absolutely guaranteed to kill or cure. I can testify. I have suffered. Simply, an onion poultice was made by cutting or otherwise mashing up a mess of cooking onions—the yellow ones—boiling them up into a thick paste and then

Auntie Bright   Doc Kistler

ladling them onto the protesting victim's chest, only a towel being protection between hot onion mess and tender hide. For a moment after the application of this boiling mush onto the cloth there was only the feeling of soothing warmth. Then the heat became almost unbearable. The victim squirmed in anguish. But the poultice was bound firm. All thoughts of illness were forgotten. If there was congestion in your chest, it was completely dispelled by this diabolical heat. You broke out into a sweat almost immediately. Of course that was the idea. The fever was broken, the congestion ended, the patient recovered.

Doc Kistler did that once to me when all else had failed and I seemed about to succumb to pneumonia. I can bear witness that the next day after the onion poultice had done its searing worst, I was ready to get up—if only so I would not suffer another one.

First Get Your Penny

When I was very little a penny and a nickel and a quarter looked alike to me. When my Uncle Charles or my Uncle Dave came to see us and they had some money to give me because I was a good boy, my father would tell me to run upstairs and fetch my bank. My bank was shiny metal. It was square and looked like the big safe in the Lytle Store, except *that* one was black with gold letters on it. There was a shiny knob on my bank, and only my father knew how to turn the knob so that the door in front would open and you could take the money out and count it. If you wanted to put money into it, there was a slot in the back. Whenever Uncle Dave or Uncle Charles gave me money, I would get my bank and put the money in the slot. Then the bank would rattle when you shook it, so that you knew the money was in there safe all right.

It wasn't until I was in first grade that I found out what money was for. It was to buy things with. Up to that time whenever I wanted candy or a rubber ball or something like that I would ask my mother, and she would buy it for me when we were "over town." But when I started school there was a store right across from the school. Always there was a little store across from a school. Always it was an old woman who kept store. We knew she was real old because she was fat and had gray hair. The woman in the store across from the Second Street School—that was the school I went to—was "Mammy" Bettinger. There was another woman who had a candy store too. That was closer to my house, and when I got a penny and wanted to spend it right away, I always ran over to her store. Her name was Mrs. Bakey.

In Mrs. Bakey's store there were two glass cases. They had shiny nickel rims around the glass. The side glass was sort of bent and low enough so that if you stood on tiptoe, you could see what was inside.

But first you had to get your penny.

The easiest way to get a penny was just to run up to your mother and ask for it. Sometimes you got it. My friend George used to run in and ask his grandma for a penny. She would tell him to go look in her pocketbook. He used to do this and get a penny. Then one day he saw there were nickels and dimes and quarters in the pocketbook, and so the next time his grandma told him to look in her pocketbook for a penny, he took out a dime. And his grandma never noticed it. Well, George had quite a good thing going; he used to get a lot of money, and all of us kids had a good time eating candy. Then one day his grandma caught on to him and what he was doing, and she told his father. George got a good licking with a strap, and his father put him in the garret. George had to spend what was left of the summer there up in the hot garret. He could only come down to eat his meals and to sleep. We used to climb on the roof of our ironworks factory shed and talk to George and play games with him. They were silly games like guessing what we had in our hands and like that. But then we would get tired and run away to play some other game, and George had no one to play with.

I guess he learned a lesson, for he never took any more money and grew up to be a very quiet boy. He was graduated from High School and went away to Germany in World War I where he was killed. Now there is a flag on his grave in Mt. Peace Cemetery every Decoration Day. They say the flags are on heroes' graves. Maybe George was a hero. I just remember that he was my friend.

But you could get pennies running errands. That was the standard reward for running an errand. You may have had to go a block or a half mile. Maybe you carried a note and had to bring back a lot of stuff the lady who got the note would give you.

I used to get a penny for going over to Zapf's big brewery to get some brewer's yeast. The brewery was back of the Zapf house on Sunbury Street. That was the main street of our town. In back of the big red brick house was the brewery, with engines and pumps and big vats and kegs and bundles of oak staves to make the kegs with. Mr. Zapf made beer and porter, and he had big delivery wagons pulled by two big dray horses. I didn't like beer, and the porter was terrible bitter. Will Zapf gave me a taste of porter once. He roared laughing when I spit it out.

When you went for yeast you had a little white china pitcher that held maybe a pint. Will Zapf would let you go back with him into a cave cut into the solid rock side of Peach Mountain back of the engine room and there were great vats of foaming stuff and that was the yeast. He would take a big dipper and get some and pour it into your pitcher. Then he would take some of the foam off the yeast in the pitcher and put a mustache on your face with it. It smelled good. And you knew that the bread and the doughnuts your mother would make with that yeast were going to smell and taste a lot better.

You could get pennies for rags and bones and old iron and "doggie diamonds." Doggie diamonds were what dogs did, but only the white ones were worth anything. They said they were used to make morocco leather, whatever that was. Paddy the Jew bought the rags and bones and such from us. He had a rickety old wagon and a horse that was skinny and old. My father used to say that the horse looked more like junk than the stuff in the wagon. Paddy the Jew would sit on an old seat made out of a board with an old piece of carpet on it. The horse would shamble along the street and Paddy the Jew would call in a sort of tired sounding singsong: "Any raaags, booones, ol' iron?"

You had been waiting all morning for Paddy the Jew and you came running out in the street as soon as you heard him. Gyp, my dog, used to run out too and sit quivering, waiting to bark at Paddy the Jew's scarecrow horse but knowing I would scold him if he did.

You would have your express wagon all filled with pieces of iron and old pipe and maybe some lead and some old bottles and some old rags your mother didn't want any more and maybe some old carpet or curtains. Paddy the Jew would look at your prizes and would moan: "That all you got? Ain't worth nuthin'." And he would cluck to his horse and make believe he was going to drive on. You would yell at him: "It's worth five cents and you know it!" Paddy the Jew would pull back on the reins and say: "Give you two cents." And you would take the two pennies that he fished out of a dirty old purse. You knew you hadn't made the best bargain in the world but two pennies was more than no pennies at all.

And what could we get with the pennies?

In Mrs. Bakey's candy store there were licorice sticks and licorice shoestrings and long licorice straps with dots of colored sugar candy on them. There were red hearts and you got them a little wooden measure for a penny. Sourballs were two for a penny. Peppermints were two for a penny. There was a magic sort of candy ball that you sucked it and every time you took it out of your mouth to look at it, it would be a different color. And each time you sucked it, it would turn another color, maybe sometimes mud color from dirty fingers. They cost a penny apiece. Hershey kisses were five for a penny. Ice cream drops were two for a penny. Nonpariels —chocolate wafers with candy sprinkles on them—were five for a penny. Old fashioneds—chocolate coated creams—

were two for a penny. Molasses coconut strips were a penny apiece. There were sugar-glazed drops that were filled with flavored water and had a marshmallow base. It was rumored that in lucky ones you would find a penny in the bottom. I never did. At Easter time there were candy eggs for a penny or five cents or a dime. Of course over at Geanslen's the Easter eggs cost more but maybe they were better. Then there were "fried eggs"—they were in a little fluted tin pan. The pan was filled with white candy with two yellow dots on it. There was a tin spoon to eat it with. They were a penny.

Up at Mammy Bettinger's you could buy moshey which was chewy molasses taffy; a hunk cost a penny. And colored fizzy powder you put in a glass of water to drink.

A penny could buy a soft pretzel. This was a pretzel about six inches long with thick and thin parts. The thin parts were the parts that crossed and they were crispy. The rest of the pretzel was like a soft bread with coarse salt sprinkled on it. An old man used to have a basket of these pretzels on his arm and we used to buy them when we went back to school after noonday lunch at home. They were still warm when we got them.

For a penny too you could buy a waffle with powdered sugar on it. The waffles were cooked while you waited. The man had a cart, with glass sides. There was a coal oil stove with a waffle iron on it. He would pour out the waffle batter and bake it and sprinkle it all over with powdered sugar and you would eat it while it was hot and gooey.

The penny ice cream man brought ice cream done up in little cubes about an inch on a side. There was vanilla and chocolate and strawberry. The cubes were wrapped in wax paper and were packed in an ice cream tub, with ice packed around. The ice cream man would drive slowly along the street and would sing; "Ice cream, penny a cake, eat it without a plate or a spoon. ICE cream . . . who'll want my ICE cream? PENNY A CAKE!"

S. Gilman

Gyp, my dog, always got to lick the paper.

That summer after I had been to school for a whole year and I had found out what pennies were good for, I lived high. I found out a way to get the door of my bank open with one of my mother's hairpins. With the door open, my wealth was exposed. To make the story short, I lived happily all summer, my buddies too, on my thefts from myself.

It was Thanksgiving Day before the awful truth came out.

My Uncle Dave and Aunt Mary came down from Ashland for Thanksgiving dinner.

Uncle Dave said: "William, where's your bank? I have something for you."

"Run get your bank, William," said my father.

I did not run. My feet dragged on the stairs. I knew the day of reckoning was at hand. I knew it was judgement day.

I brought the bank to my Uncle Dave. It didn't rattle.

My father looked at me. He took the bank. He shook it. It didn't rattle for him either.

I had to confess.

A Bone for Gyp

Once I heard my father say to my mother: "Fannie, you are a lucky woman. You have the whole world brought right to your door!"

I thought this was funny talk because I knew the world was bigger than Minersville, just as Pottsville was bigger than Minersville and Philadelphia was bigger than Pottsville. I knew how big those places were, and I knew there was a lot more of the world than I had ever seen. I learned that in my big yellow geography book (the one we used to hide our nickel novels behind).

My mother said: "I think I'd like to have Wanamaker's at my door instead."

That made sense, because I had been in Wanamaker's Store. It was in Philadelphia, and we used to go down there sometimes to buy things. The 8:15 train took us down, and we got the 4:35 back in the afternoon. Wanamaker's store had a big place on the first floor where you could sit when you were tired. There were flags hung all around, and there was a big organ which a man played every so often. People from the coal regions and from the Pennsy Dutch country around Berks County used to meet other friends there in the big court. It was something like Siegel and Cooper's in New York. My grandpa took me there once. There they had palm trees all around, and you could buy ice cream. They used to say "Meet me at the fountain"—they meant real flowing-water fountain.

But I made out that my father didn't mean that the whole world itself was going to come to Minersville. He meant that almost anything we wanted to eat came to the door for us.

First, there was August Scheiffle. He was a big man, with

a red face and a mustache. In summer he wore a straw hat. He was the butcher. He had a big wagon covered with shining white oilcloth. A big black horse with a long mane and a long shiny tail pulled it. Mr. Scheiffle sat in front to drive and to cut and weigh the meats and things.

He had a chopping block, and his cleaver, meat saw, and knives were on a rack. In the back of the wagon, on scoured wood slats were his meats covered with clean white cheese-cloth to keep the flies off. He had beef, pork, veal, and sometimes lamb. My father never ate lamb, and he wouldn't let my mother buy any. I never tasted lamb until I was grown up. I think my father was so kind-hearted he couldn't bear to think of the little woolly lambs being killed to eat. I didn't think much of the idea either, though I shot sparrows with my air rifle. There was a lamb in one of the windows of our Lutheran church. He looked so meek and mild that no one would ever kill him. Jesus was the Lamb.

Mr. Scheiffle had baloney and liver and kidneys and hearts and such things. The liver and the hearts and kidneys didn't cost much—maybe five cents or so a pound. But the baloney cost more—about 15 cents a pound. It was awfully good. Mr. Scheiffle made it himself.

Every time Mr. Scheiffle came to our house he blew on a horn, and my mother would come out to get her meat. But she never got to the wagon first. My dog Gyp and my cat Fritz were tied for first; I was there second. My mother always had to stop to put on her sunbonnet or her shawl. Women are like that. They always have to put something on.

There was always a piece of baloney for me. It was cut sort of slantwise on the roll, so the piece was bigger than as if you had cut right across. Gyp used to sit up and beg, and Mr. Scheiffle would give him a bone. Fritz knew he'd get some liver, so he just sat there waiting. He didn't do any tricks. He was smart.

We never got any samples like that from Mr. Reiss. You

AUGUST SCHEIFLE
FINE MEATS

S. Gilman

couldn't eat his stuff because it wasn't cooked. Unless you wanted to eat oysters raw. Some people did. And people paid for the oysters that they ate raw. They would have had to pay me. Mr. Reiss—Johnny Reiss, everybody called him—got his oysters from the Chesapeake Bay and his fish from the big nets off the coast of New Jersey. You could get the oysters in the shells, or he would open them and put them in a pail my mother would bring out with her. She made stew with them.

He used to cut the heads and tails and fins off the fish and clean and scale then right on the wagon. He wasn't as neat as Mr. Scheiffle. Or maybe the flies liked fish more. He used to throw a fishhead to Fritz, but I didn't want anything, especially not a raw oyster, and Gyp agreed with me. He sold tartar sauce and cole slaw and home made mustard relish that went with fish.

Mr. Schwenk came all the way from the Tzummer Bareck—Summer Mountain—with his farm produce wagon. He brought all kinds of farm things like chickens, potatoes, beans, corn, salad, egg plants, carrots, and beets. He brought apples, peaches, plums, and grapes when they were in season. Whatever he grew on his farm he brought to Minersville when in season.

Another farmer used to come to our house, but I never knew his name. I know he lived away over in Deep Creek across the Broad Mountain—maybe five or six miles from Minersville.

He was an old, old man with shaggy hair and hair in his ears. Because he was beanpole thin, my mother used to say that he must live on apples. That was all he used to bring. Apples. They were poor apples—wormy, but mother used to buy some because she pitied him. He had a boy who rode with him on the wagon. The wagon was as old as the old man, rattley and shaky; and was pulled by a horse whose bones just about stuck through his hide. The horse could hardly pull the wagon, he was so old. The boy told my mother once that they used to have a nice farm, but the black water from the mines had drowned it with culm—coal dirt—one year. All they had left was part of the orchard. He said his mother was dead and this was his grandfather.

One day they came to our place with apples. But instead of the old wagon they had a little cart, almost as worn out as the old wagon was. They had pulled it themselves, all the way from Deep Creek, six miles over the Broad Mountain!

My mother out of pity bought some apples, although she had to throw them away because they were so wormy. She asked them where the horse was, and the old man shook his head and said in Pennsy Dutch: "He died." The little boy said, quietly: "Last week." He sort of sniffled. That was the last time they ever came to our house with apples. Maybe the old man died, too.

Mr. Dieruff was another man who stopped at our house. He was called George. He sold all kinds of pickles and smoked sausage and summer sausage, horseradish, all kinds of relishes, scrapple, and cornmeal mush for frying. He had sauerkraut, too, but my mother always made her own. After she cut the cabbage on a slaw board she put it down in a big crock. A layer of cabbage, then some salt, then another layer of cabbage and more salt. She put a plate and a big stone on top for weight and covered the crock with cheesecloth. The crock was kept in the cool cellar, and in about a week the cabbage was soured. There was a lot of brine water to keep it from spoiling. Mr. Dieruff had schmierkäse (called cottage cheese now) that was smooth as silk as it was spread on bread.

My father always used to keep the apple butter dish and the schmierkäse dish far apart on our table when my "Auntie" Bright came to clean our house once a week. She did our washing, too. We used to pay her a dollar. Well, "Auntie" Bright used to put schmierkäse on her bread along with apple butter with the same knife. Soon you couldn't tell which was which, and my father didn't like that.

The corn we got from the farmer was mostly shoepeg. It was white corn and good for eating off the cob—if you didn't have false teeth—or for cutting off and creaming. We bought bushels of shoepeg in late summer, and "Auntie" Bright would cut it off the cobs, spread it on flat tin sheets for drying in the oven. Then she poured the dried corn into muslin bags that five pounds of sugar came in and hung them up in the garret for winter. When the corn was soaked in water it was just like fresh, except it had a sort of smoky taste. She dried blackberries and peaches too, And of course made schnitz.

Schnitz were for schnitz pie and for schnitz und knepf. You made schnitz by paring apples, coring them, and cutting them into eighths. The women used a little machine which would spear the apple on a tined holder. As a crank was turned the holder took out the core and a knife blade cut off the skin. The apple pieces were dried in the oven and bagged to be put in the garret for the winter. So we had dried apples, blackberries, and peaches for pies all winter. All you had to do with schnitz was to soak them in water over night, and they were like fresh apples. Schnitz und knepf was my favorite. Mother would take a ham hock and put it in a pot with the soaked schnitz. Along about the time the schnitz were well plumped up from boiling, she would make the knepf (dumplings) out of flour, water, and eggs. Globs of the knepf were floated on the boiling ham-apple water. Then when the dumplings were done we had a feast. And maybe we would have schnitz pie for dessert.

Other people came to our door to sell things. The Healena Salve man used to come. He charged 25 cents for his salve. It was butter yellow and smelled of carbolic acid. It was good for almost anything you needed a salve for—burns and bruises and things like that. There was another salve that

was called "Old Woman's Salve". That came in flat tins like
the Healena. It was sort of blackish and smelled pretty good.

In the summer time little "foreign" boys used to come to
the door to sell huckleberries. The mines didn't work much
in the summer, and the "foreigners" used to go up in the
mountains and strip the berries from the low bushes. Then
the children would walk the two or three miles to Minersville
to sell them for ten cents a quart. Late in the afternoon, if
they hadn't sold all their huckleberries, they began to cry
real tears as they tried to sell the berries for three quarts for
a quarter. Once we even got them for five cents a quart. The
berries were full of sticks and leaves, but they were blue and
sweet and made good pies.

My father liked huckleberry pie. But he had false teeth.
That was the only time I ever saw him without his teeth. He
would look at the juicy pie, all beautiful dark blue, hot from
the oven and would excuse himself as he left the table. He
returned with his cheeks caved in to "gum" the pie and
smack his lips over it.

When I needed a new suit either Mr. Oerther or Mr.
Schloss would come to our house. Both of them ran haberdashery stores, and my father was a friend to both. So one
time Mr. Schloss would come and another time Mr.
Oerther.

They brought tape measures and pictures along with little
pieces of cloth they called swatches, to show the kinds of
cloth you could get in your suit. Most times I got blue serge
because that wore best of all. Your pants got real shiny
though. They sent the measurements down to tailors in Philadelphia. When the suit arrived there would be a shiny new
penny in one of the pockets. A belt or a pair of suspenders
came free. You could make a choice yourself. I always took
the belt.

Not all my clothes came from the Minersville merchants.
We used to go to Brooklyn, New York, for vacations in

summer time. My grandma and grandpa Harris lived in Brooklyn at 1164 Fulton Street. On the first floor was the shop of Mr. Muchmore the florist. He lived with his blonde wife on the second floor. My grandma and grandpa and two of my uncles lived on the third floor, which was level with the elevated railroad. It was fun to watch the trains go by. They had little red engines to pull them the first years I saw them. After that the cars were run by electricity. On the top floor was Mr. and Mrs. Pratt. They were deaf and dumb, and only my grandma knew what they were saying with their hands. She could talk hand signs with them.

Well, when my mother and I went to Brooklyn, she and my grandma used to take me to the big department stores, like Abraham-Strauss. They were a lot bigger than the stores in Pottsville, but not as big as Wanamaker's.

My mother used to see things in the Brooklyn department stores which she bought for me. This was a terrible mistake, but she didn't know that. The trouble was that the styles in Brooklyn were about two years ahead of the styles in the coal regions. So when I went back to Minersville and had to wear these city clothes and things I was marked for life. I mean one time I had to dress up in a Buster Brown outfit with a hat with a big wide brim and ribbon. It had knicker-bockers when everyone else was wearing straight pants. That was just awful. And then one time my mother bought me a winter coat in Brooklyn. It had a fur collar. No one had fur collars in Minersville, not even the rich people. The first time that I wore it I came home and my nose was bleeding. I had drops of blood on the fur, and my mother screamed "What's happened?" And I said I bumped into a fence, but I really bumped into Clint Mervine's fist when we had a hassle because he called me Santa Claus.

I didn't like Brooklyn clothes. They weren't worth fighting for.

Gettysburg's Last Casualty

In school we were all deathly afraid of Mr. Henry Haak Spayd.

Mr. Henry Haak Spayd, also known to us as Mr. H. H. Spayd, and to the older boys in high school as "Ol' Spade 'n' Shovel" (behind his back, of course), was superintendent of our public schools. He was a veteran of the Civil War and lived his disciplined Army days all the rest of his life. He believed implicitly the adage, "Spare the rod and spoil the child." His favorite instrument of discipline was a lath about three feet long, a half inch thick, and two inches wide.

When he came around to visit a school room—and that he did a lot—the drop of a pin would have sounded like the boom of a cannon at Gettysburg.

Strangely enough, Mr. Henry Haak Spayd was the last casualty of the Battle of Gettysburg.

We called it Decoration Day. On the 30th day of May we honored our hero dead—those who had fought in the Revolutionary War, the Mexican War, the Civil War, and the War with Spain. We still had a veteran of the Mexican War in our county. I saw him once. In a parade he sat ramrod stiff on a big black horse. His name was Col. James Nagle, and he fought in the Civil War too. He was a colonel of the 48th Pennsylvania Volunteer Infantry—my great uncle Samuel's regiment.

Decoration Day was a day of prayer, a day of reverence and of homage. I daresay fewer people died on that day than on any other holiday. It wasn't a holiday, but a Holy Day. It was a quiet day, no picnics, no outings. No one tried to go from here to there in a hurry. No one tried to leap into a new grave. We just took the day to pay our respects and our

59

love to those who were in their last resting places leaving the full memory that they had done their best, when their best was called for.

The day before Decoration Day, if it came during the week, we were let out of school an hour early for our midday meal. That was to give us time to pick flowers to decorate the graves. We brought our flowers back to school with us in the afternoon.

A tomato can was our usual container. We filled it with water and put our flowers in it. In late May there would be "flags"—yellow, and blue, and white iris. Mostly the flags were blue. Mountain laurel was just coming to bloom, and its sticky white and pinkish white blossoms contrasted beautifully with the dark waxy green leaves. Then there might be some lilacs left on the shady side of the house. Brown-eyed Susans just might be blooming. Snowballs were. And there was mock orange, though the petals soon fell. That didn't make any difference to us. They looked beautiful. If you couldn't find anything else, there were always the brave little yellow dandelions.

We almost ran back to school, because we knew the treat that was ahead for us—a program in our school and then a visit to the Grand Army Hall on Third Street, back of Lawrence's store.

All the cans of flowers were put up front in school. The year that I remember best was the first year I had Alice Robins for a teacher. That was in sub-grammar school—grades five and six. I was just finishing my fifth grade.

After all the flowers had been arranged to Miss Robins' liking, we had our Decoration Day program. Miss Robins told us about the day and why we must always keep it sacred in our hearts. She told us how her own brother had gone off to war and had died at Antietam. Then she asked each one of us whether we had a dead hero in our families. I guess half a dozen of us raised our hands. When it came time for me to tell about my hero I was so excited that I could hardly remember his name.

"My hero was my great uncle Samuel," I finally blurted. "He was a captain in the infantry, and he commanded one of the first companies of Negro soldiers ever to fight on the Union side in the War. He went away to Indianapolis to take command of the men and brought them all the way back east to the Army of the Potomac that General Grant was to command. After turning them over to another captain he went back to his regiment—the 48th Pennsylvania.

"He was in the battles around Richmond and was killed by a Rebel sharpshooter at Tolpohotamy Creek. The sharpshooter hit him in the neck, and he died in about four days. My grandfather went all the way down to Virginia after the war and brought his body back for burial in Schuylkill Haven."

Having done my share, and the rest having testified to the toll of war, Miss Robins said it would be nice for us to pray for all those brave men. She made up a prayer, just like the minister does in church. She said something like this, as she bowed her head, and so did we: "Dear Lord, please, we ask you to remember the dead from our little town. Let them be happy in Your heaven. May all their wounds be healed and their bodies made whole so that they may no longer bear the scars of cruel war. May their hearts be made whole also, so that they may each love one another and love those on the Confederate side who died for a cause they too thought just. And may those left on this earth to mourn always keep the day we call Decoration Day solemn and holy. Bring us that day into Your churches. Bring us into Your graveyards. Help us all to bow our heads and pray as Your Son taught us: 'Our Father which art in heaven, hallowed be Thy name. Thy kingdom come. Thy will be done on earth as it is in heaven. Give us this day our daily bread. And forgive us our trespasses as we forgive those who trespass against us. And lead us not into temptation, but deliver us from evil: for Thine is the Kingdom and the power and the glory forever and ever. Amen.' "

Miss Robins stood with her eyes closed for maybe a minute after we had finished the Lord's Prayer. Then she opened her eyes and blew her nose, took off her steel-rimmed spectacles and dabbed at her eyes. Then she swallowed a couple of times and called for the first speaker on our program.

The girls were the best speakers, but some of the boys were good too. One boy could deliver Robert Emmet's Oration. I never could speak a half dozen words in front of an audience without making a fool of myself. My recitations were always the shortest I could find. I never spoke a piece on Decoration Day. There just weren't any short enough for me to remember.

Nellie Yoder was our best speaker. She used gestures just like the orators on the Fourth of July. They were called the Delsarte gestures, my mother said. There was a gesture for everything—from happiness to deep grief, from love to hate, from resignation to deep remorse, from sobriety to drunkenness.

We used to snicker when Nellie got up to make a speech. That wasn't very kind. Nellie had been a victim of a most horrible experience when she made a speech in a Christmas program two years before. Her piece was "Twinkle, Twinkle, Little Star." She was in Maria Brennan's room that year, and Miss Brennan thought that it would be nice if everyone on the program had a costume. Nellie's was a band of crinkly red crepe paper around her forehead. On it was pasted gold stars. She wore a silver crown on her head and held a wand wrapped in red tissue paper with a gold star at the tip. She looked beautiful.

It was unfortunate that Nellie, gripped with the fervor of her piece, began to perspire. Only we called it sweat. As Nellie spoke, making grand gestures with her wand, little runlets of red began to streak her cheeks. We began to titter as Nellie became a painted Indian with blond hair right before our eyes. When a final streak ran down her nose from bridge to tip, we busted our sides laughing. Nellie only made matters worse by rubbing her hand across her face, smearing the gorgeous striped effect. Poor Miss Brennan called a halt to the program. Nellie, in tears, was taken to the side of the room where the water bucket stood, and Miss Brennan washed her face.

But on the Decoration Day I'm telling about, Nellie was more grown up. She was sure of herself now and stood there and recited "The Blue and the Grey." Solemnly she said— no gestures now—"Under the sod and the dew, waiting the Judgement Day, under the laurel the Blue, under the willow the Grey."

I tell you, we were the ones who had tears in our eyes.

After the program, we marched two by two to Grand Army Hall with our flowers. When we got there we put the cans on the floor along with the flowers other schools had brought. My Uncle Joe Levan was there and showed us all the battle flags from the 48th Pennsylvania, the regimental drum and bugle, and the guidons that only brave men could carry, for they were in the front of the fight because the colored guidons kept the companies together in line of battle even when there was a charge. If a color bearer was shot down, there was always another brave soldier to pick up the guidon and carry it high.

We knew that on Decoration Day the Patriotic Order of Sons of America, the United Sons of Veterans of the Civil War, and the United Spanish War Veterans would take the flowers to the cemeteries around our town. We would hear the sad notes of the buglers blowing Taps and the crash of the three volleys from the rifles.

Mr. Spayd was at the Grand Army Hall. He was usually marshal of the Decoration Day parade. He had been a color bearer in the war and had fought at Gettysburg. Years later, the United Press International carried a dispatch that related the last chapter in Mr. Spayd's long life. It read:

"Oct. 19, 1927 was the date. The day was gray and dripping and cold in Washington, D.C. The rain let up as President Calvin Coolidge, escorted by a troop of cavalry, left the White House. The procession went to a spot near the Botanical Gardens below Capitol Hill. There, in a setting of rippling flags and Civil War Corps shields, ringed by soldiers, sailors, and marines, a crowd had gathered for the unveiling of a monument to Maj. Gen. George Gordon Meade, Union commander at Gettysburg.

"And with the speakers on the platform was a man who had been a color bearer at the Battle of Gettysburg, Henry Haak Spayd, past commander of the Pennsylvania G.A.R.

"Miss Henrietta Meade, the General's daughter, who was 10 when the battle was fought, was present, wearing a big corsage. As she pulled the line, unveiling the monument, a field artillery unit fired a 13-gun salute and 48 pigeons, representing Peace, were released.

"Coolidge then accepted the monument in a long scholarly address. Then Spayd arose to deliver 'Reminiscences of General Meade.' He was in his 83rd year. A reporter who was there recalls: 'The old man was transported back to the field of battle as he spoke. He was an erect, slight old fellow. Wore a campaign hat, turned up on one side. As he told about the fighting, he would point to various sectors, describing the Rebs deployment, the fierceness of the attack, and the terrain. Finally, with a gesture somewhat to his right, he told of a barn, a red barn. There was a hell of a fight going on in connection with that barn. As the old man told of the fighting, memory's bullets began to whiz around his head. I could almost hear them myself. He dropped to one knee, then took cover behind an imaginary something.

" 'As his story of the battle waxed and waned, it became

the battle in fact. The old man was as surely returned to the field of Gettysburg as it is possible for mind to triumph over matter. He spoke and shouted about the barn. He noted rebel hits and the death or wounding of his buddies on either side. It became mighty strange. After some minutes, Coolidge's physician stepped up to the edge of the stage and gently talked the old man away from the long gone war.

" 'His was the last talk, and a heavy shower started as he was led away, to be taken to the Old Soldier's Home. He died in a few hours. Those Reb sharpshooters had picked him off at a distance of nearly 100 miles and nearly 65 years later. He was the last battle casualty of Gettysburg.' "

What Mr. Spayd was describing was the fight to dislodge Confederate sharpshooters from the Bliss barn, which stood between Ziegler's Grove and the town of Gettysburg. Zieg-

Second Street School

ler's Grove stood not far from the curve of the famous "Fishhook" position of the Union Army.

In the barn were sharpshooters and expert riflemen of the Confederacy who were picking off Union soldiers on the crest of Cemetery Hill, at the Grove not far from Rickett's Battery. They were making so much trouble the men in blue decided to end it by taking the barn. They succeeded in their attack. It was a minor part of the great battle, but it was one of fierce action. It was called off because Union commanders sensed that the Rebs were about to make a supreme effort to win the general engagement—the effort known as Pickett's Charge. No wonder Mr. Spayd actually relived the scene as he described it.

We didn't know, in those days that were, that Mr. H. H. Spayd would one day meet his Maker in such a dramatic fashion. For us he was the man who would lead the marchers in the solemn Decoration Day parade.

Dynamiting the Fourth of July

There were three nights in the year when we kids really prayed.

Of course we said our "Now I lay me's" every night. But the nights before the Fourth of July, the Sunday School picnic, and Christmas, we really got down to hard knocks and prayed our little hearts out right direct to God himself.

The night before the Fourth we prayed that the dynamiters wouldn't rock the sky so hard it would pour for the big day.

That dynamiting was pure torture. We all knew that thunder brought down rain from the clouds. It was absolutely positive that dynamite blasts were louder than thunderclaps. The ear-shattering blasts on the eve of the Fourth could only result in one horrible happening—it would rain on the Fourth.

Seven hills surrounded our little coal mining town in eastern Pennsylvania.

For weeks the miners overdrew their allotment of blasting dynamite. By twilight on "the night before" there was enough high explosive stacked carelessly atop the seven hills to blow our entire town into the hereafter.

The first blast came just at dusk. From then on until midnight the hills rocked in an inferno of explosions. Blast followed shuddering blast. Orange flashes gave the sky a constant hell-fire glow. Shockwaves from the explosions rocked houses, brought down plaster, even broke windows.

It was awe-inspiring. It was hell on earth. It was glorious. It was frightening—and for us kids it was pure torture.

There was no thought of sleep while the bombardment lasted. Quarter sticks, half sticks, sometimes a whole stick of

67

dynamite went off. At midnight the seven hills erupted like so many volcanoes. You expected red hot lava to descend on the town. Then there was silence, like peace at the end of a war. Then God must have heard our fervent: "Please God, don't let it rain tomorrow." That it was already "today" by some minutes didn't occur to us.

That prayer brings results was amply demonstrated. I don't remember one Fourth of July that didn't dawn clear, with promise of a splendid day to follow.

The band woke us up at 5 a.m. The Minersville Silver Cornet Band, led by Charles Clappier, was atop Kear's Hill, highest of the seven. The first tune they played was "Columbia the Gem of the Ocean!"

Father, mother, and I stood at the open front bedroom window and listened to the tunes a soft July breeze carried to us. "America," "The Battle Hymn of the Republic," "There'll Be a Hot Time in the Old Town Tonight," "Tenting Tonight," "John Brown's Body Lies Amouldering in the Grave," "The Star Spangled Banner."

It was past six when the last notes died away.

After breakfast father gave me money to buy fireworks, and I had saved some of my own too. My little pocket book was stuffed with nickles and dimes and quarters—and one whole dollar bill! I went over to Will Jones' store on Sunbury Street.

There all the books, tablet paper, pencils, magazines, and newspapers were shoved to one side, and there were rows and rows of fire crackers—cannon crackers, lady crackers, salutes, pinwheels, mines, rockets, roman candles, shooting stars, fountains, snakes, torpedoes, devil crackers, red fire— and sparklers for the girls.

You could buy shooting canes—you put a .22 calibre blank at the tip end and when you banged the tip on the sidewalk there was a satisfying explosion.

Lady crackers cost a penny a pack. You set those off a

string at a time. Regular firecrackers were a nickel or a dime, depending on the size of the red pack and the size of the crackers. They had strange looking gold or red labels pasted on them—all in Chinese. Cannon crackers and salutes could cost as much as ten cents apiece. Torpedoes were a nickel a box, and they came packed in sawdust. You threw them on the pavement to explode them. You put a devil cracker on the walk and stamped on it, and it flashed into little bits. Each one would explode in a blue flame when you stamped on them. A couple kids with a half dozen devil crackers could raise quite a racket.

Will Jones would sell the big salutes only to the older boys. Some people said there was dynamite in them. But I took one apart, and it had only black powder in it like the others. We put the powder in a pile and made a powder train to it and touched it with glowing punk; we almost set our back porch afire. You bought sticks of punk to light your firecrackers with. The punk sticks were brown and a little thinner than a lead pencil. It was lit with a match or from another stick of punk that was burning. You blew on the lighted end until it got a good red glow on it. A stick of punk would last about a half hour. You could buy incense punk to keep mosquitoes off, too. They were thinner and had a sliver of bamboo in them.

Mines were cylinder shaped things of cardboard covered with red paper. There was a fuse on top. When a mine went off, colored balls shot out of it, and finally there would be a big explosion and a lot of colored fireballs blew high in the air. A little mine cost a nickel, but big ones could cost as much as a half dollar. I wasn't allowed to have big ones. Only my father dared set these off. And the same for sky-rockets and roman candles. These were for night time use, anyhow, along with red fire and fountains. My father would come over town with me and buy fireworks for our big display after dark. We always had the best display in the neighborhood—until one year a roman candle shot up my father's sleeve, and a skyrocket went under our porch. That was the end of our public displays.

But, when you bought your firecrackers, dark was a long way off, and you ran back home with your firecrackers and stored them safe so they all wouldn't go off at once. You shot firecrackers off in singles, or you could twist two fuses together and set two off at a time. Sometimes you put one under a tin can, and when it went off, it would blow the can way up in the air. Then if you dared, you could light one and hold it in your hand until the fuse was almost burned to the powder and then throw it into the air to explode. Those without fuses were broken in half so that the bent halves faced each other. You then touched off your punk to the powder, and they fought each other, with flames shooting out.

The Fourth of July parade was set for ten o'clock in the morning.

By that time most of us had squandered all our firecrackers for the day. Some of us were thrifty enough to divide our store and save half for the afternoon. At any rate, by the time we all went over to Sunbury Street for the parade, it was inches deep in the red paper firecracker covers, and big salutes were blasting the paper into red blizzards.

My dog Gyp wasn't allowed to go with me to see the parade. Gyp had a natural hatred for things that went bang, like fire crackers, and he tried his best to put a stop to the whole racket. He would rush out for a firecracker and grab it and shake it. Most time the firecracker went off in his mouth. By eight o'clock all his whiskers were gone—burned off—and my father would take pity on him and say: "William, I think you'd better put Gyp in the cellar before he gets his head blown off." Gyp knew he was to be banished. He just sort of moaned when we took him to the cellar door and pushed him toward the steps. Later in the day, when most of

Father Sets Off Fireworks

the noise had died down, we let him out. He would be trembling all over, but his taste for firecrackers would be somewhat dulled. My cat Fritz was wise. He just found a nice cool place in the cellar, all by himself and slept all day.

Everybody came out to see the parade. They came from all the mining patches. The new immigrants, most of them, had never seen a parade American style. They were used to soldiers and guns and mounted cavalry. But our parades were different. They formed up something like this:

>Grand Marshal on horseback
>Color guard
>Grand Army of the Republic veterans in carriages
>Minersville Silver Cornet Band, Charles Clappier, bandmaster and leader.
>Patriotic Order Sons of America
>United Spanish War Veterans, on foot
>Sons of Veterans of the Civil War
>Our Boys Band, Charles Wagner director
>Mountaineer Steam Fire Engine, holiday dress
>Mountaineer Fire Company, in uniform
>Good Will Hook and Ladder Truck, holiday dress
>Good Will Fire Company, in uniform
>Independence Hose Cart, holiday dress
>Independence Fire Company, in uniform
>Rescue Hook and Ladder Truck, holiday dress
>Rescue Hook and Ladder Company, in uniform
>Santa Barbara Society Marching Band, Caesar Romano, director
>Santa Barbara Italian Society
>Marching Veterans from Foreign Lands, in native uniforms

Floats:

>Uncle Tom Tableaux—Uncle Tom Scourged by Simon Legree
>Eliza Escaping Across the Ice

Lincoln Freeing the Slaves
The Coal Miner
Liberty Enlightening the World
Boating at Tumbling Run
A Summer Picnic
The Evils of Strong Drink

Everybody cheered as the Grand Army Veterans rode by in decorated open carriages. All wore their GAR uniforms, wearing their little blue caps on graying heads. There were about twenty-five in line of march.

The Minersville Silver Cornet Band always had the place of honor as first band in the parade. Their blue uniforms had a military cut. Our Boys Band was made up of boys from Minersville, trained by "Spoony" Wagner, haberdashery merchant. They wore khaki uniforms, some of which fit. Santa Barbara's leader was nicknamed "Duckfoot"; he brought his big feet down in marching cadence, the while flourishing his silver trumpet like a band major's baton.

The Mountaineer Steamer had its fire roaring, with Franz Kraus the stoker. Smoke belched from the polished nickle stack. Brasswork shone like gold. A team of big blacks drew the engine, a fireman at the head of each horse. Red and white bunting decorated the wheels, as it did the wheels of the other fire department apparatus. From time to time Franz yanked on the whistle cord and let loose an ear-splitting blast.

We all cheered the floats loudest. Everybody knew the participants.

George Huffman was a wiry, thin Simon Legree, complete with "villain" whiskers, flailing away at cringing Andy Burke as Uncle Tom. They were in front of a replica of Uncle Tom's cabin, made of real pine logs. Back of the cabin was the scene where Minnie Beck, as Eliza, was running across the ice. The ice was real, courtesy of Geanslen's

Ice Cream Company, and Minnie, no fool she, had had mind enough to wear her winter boots and leggings.

The tallest man in town was blacksmith Adam Hinkel. With a towering stove pipe hat, he made Lincoln look seven feet tall. He held a scroll of parchment in his hands. Before him three slaves knelt before an anvil, and Joe Thomas, my father's boss mechanic, was striking off their shackles. Even with their burnt cork makeup, everyone recognized Charlie Ulmer, Jim Hoskins and Ike Dietrich as the slaves.

The Coal Miner—he was Steve Sobolewski—hacked away at a huge chunk of anthracite coal (courtesy of the Philadelphia & Reading Coal and Iron Company, Pine Knot Colliery). Steve had on his miners' felt boots, heavy trousers, and a miner's hat with the coal oil lamp lit. Helping him load the coal he had chipped off with his pick was Tad Jenkins, complete with big scoop shovel, and shoveling it into a half-filled mine buggy—also from Pine Knot.

Myrtle Griffith was our Liberty. Garbed in red, white, and blue bunting, she held aloft a silver torch with red tissue paper to imitate flames. Her fair hair spread in the breeze as she stood before a globe labeled "The World." Three little children in Russian, German, and Italian costumes knelt before her—Beth Bateman, Fannie Richards and Edith Heckman. Madelaine Strauss, Eva Gallagher, Ivy Dietz, Earl Lawrence, Maurice Edmunds, and Stanley Sheeder made up the Summer Picnic group. They lolled in a haywagon (courtesy of the Fred Zimmermann Livery Stable), the girls playing mandolins while the boys waved baseball bats and gloves.

So the parade went on. The last float was "The Evils of Strong Drink." Three girls from high school, Bessie Kaufman, Mary Bettinger, and Ida Warner, dressed in pure white, with sashes labeled "Temperance" in gold across their breasts, stood with hands outstretched before the sodden drunk with a whiskey bottle (bottle courtesy of Frank

Bender Wholesale Liquor Store). He was played by Frank Brennan. The girls offered pure mountain spring water (courtesy Minersville Water Company, Harrison Kear, president) to the fallen man. The dray carrying the impressive tableau was furnished by the Charles Zapf Brewing Company. Since they made beer, not strong drink, our morals were satisfied.

That was the parade; it was all over for another year.

Back home, on our side street, I knew what would be waiting. The day before the Fourth I had had a hand in the making of the treat. Mother had put good heavy cream, sugar, vanilla, and some beaten eggs into the big freezer and packed it with a mixture of cracked ice and coarse rock salt. I had turned the crank until my small muscles tired. Then my father took it and gave it some fast twirls, just to show how it should be done, ground away a little longer and then said: "Fannie, I think we could lick the paddle now!"

No ice cream in the whole world ever tasted as good as that which dripped from the freezer paddle when my mother had taken it out and rested it on a dinner plate. Gyp got a good taste—I dripped some cream on a paper for him.

That was the treat that waited our return from the parade. There was good home boiled ham, pickles, pickled eggs— red from beet juice and vinegar—chowchow, fresh bread, home made lemonade, layer cake and . . . the ice cream.

We rested up a bit after the good things, then we kids got to work again at celebrating the day. We hoarded our fire crackers now to make them last. It wouldn't have done any good to go over town—Jones' would be sold out.

At dusk I set off my store of small-fry fireworks—pinwheels, fountains, red fire, little roman candles. Then my father would put on his big display. All over town the big rockets and roman candles would be soaring into the air, blazing and banging. Hot air balloons, made of tissue paper and inflated by the heat from a small ball of wax-soaked excelsior, rose majestically into the night, to be watched until they disappeared from sight—hopefully not still ablaze.

The rockets became fewer. The noise died down. There were a few sparklers left, and a few pieces of glowing punk. We ran around making circles in the air with the glowing stumps of punk.

It was time to go to bed.

The Fourth of July was over.

Down Goes Aunt Lucy

My Aunt Lucy was not one to push her chair away from the dinner table. She liked her vittles, her *schnitz und knepp*, that delectable stew of ham hock, dried apples, and dumplings; her sauerkraut with mashed potatoes and good fat pork; her stewed chicken with waffles swimming in gravy; her raisin pie; three-deck layer cake with butter cream frosting; and ice cream (any flavor so long as it was vanilla).

So when she sat on the railing of the Minersville Boat House at Tumbling Run something had to happen. It did.

My friend Charlie "Fats" Wernert and I were fishing for sunnies off the boathouse porch at the time.

Charlie looked over the broken railing as Aunt Lucy disappeared in a lather of foam and a huge wave that lapped the shore furiously.

"Bubble! Bubble! Bubble!" he said, in mild interest. "Down goes Aunt Lucy!"

As long as we were kids this observation, repeated with gestures, was good for roll-on-the-ground laughs.

Aunt Lucy was fished out and dried off, and not long afterward, was doing full justice to the picnic lunch. Charlie and I ate heartily, too.

Tumbling Run was one of the more delightful places you could go to on the trolley cars.

You boarded the Tumbling Run trolley in Union Square in Pottsville and fought the other kids to get on the front seat of the open cars. That way you could see the motorman board the car with his big brass control handle and watch him fit the handle over the socket on the power box to get ready to embark. His conductor would give him a bell signal, the motorman would turn the handle, and the trolley would start to move. His foot kept up a rhythmic clanging of the bell to warn people and teams out of the way.

Two blocks after the car got under way, it flew downhill under the Philadelphia and Reading railroad tracks. That took your breath away. You were sure you were doing the speed of a Barney Oldfield—60 miles an hour, they said he did in an automobeel.

A half mile along the way it swung right over the highest iron bridge in the whole world. If you were in the front seat you were almost sorry you were there. You could see the awful depths not only to either side, but through the tracks! Those inside the car could cower together, away from the ends of the seats. That was a help. But you'd never let on you were afraid. Maybe you whistled. The motorman had to slow down crossing this enormous iron bridge. Way, way down below there was the river, the canal, and the railroad. The engines and the railroad cars looked like toys.

Once the trolley was across the bridge and the passengers had just about gotten their breath back, the motorman gave the motors more electricity to bring us to the section that we called "The Home Stretch." That was a green tunnel through the woods where the trolley went full speed lickety split to the end of the line at the Tumbling Run platform.

Everybody piled out of the car, most lugging picnic baskets. There was a merry-go-round right there and a grove with picnic tables. A steam launch took you all around the beautiful lake for five cents and would make a stop anywhere to let you off at one of the boat houses. There was a big whistle on the launch, and every so often the captain, who wore a regular captain's cap, would tug on the whistle cord, and the deep tone would echo from the mountains around the lake.

Some people said there was no bottom in the mountain-encircled lake, that springs went way down into the bowels of the earth, that you couldn't drop a measuring weight down into their swirling depths. But actually the lake was 65 feet deep at the breast of the big stone dam. My father told me that. He knew everything like that.

The lake was built to provide water for the Schuylkill Canal when the streams that fed the canal went dry. The canal started at Mt. Carbon right below the dam and flowed all the way to Philadelphia.

All along the shores of Tumbling Run Lake there were cottages, called boat houses, and each one had a name. The one we always went to was just called "The Minersville Boat House," and it was owned by Mr. George Geanslen, the ice cream maker. You could take the steam launch to get to it, or you could have some one row you over. We always took the steam launch, for when you did that you got the trip around the lake for the same money. You could have lunch on the boat house porch, and fish off the porch at the same time. We caught sunfish and little catfish there and once in a while a trout.

It cost five cents to go from Pottsville to Tumbling Run. But there were lots of other places you could go for a nickel. You could go to Railway Park on the trolley. There were picnic tables and a dance floor and a shelter in case it rained.

The Steam Launch Took You All Around the Lake for Five Cents

We had our Sunday School picnic there once. I didn't like it much because I was catcher and got hit on the head by a bat. It knocked me out, and my head was cut open. A lot of girls came around and tried to make my head stop hurting, but they didn't do much good.

It only cost a nickel to go from Minersville to Pottsville to shop in the big stores there—Dives, Pomeroy and Stewart's, or Miehle's. They were just as good as the Philadelphia stores, only they weren't as big. The best thing about going to Pottsville to shop was that after you had all your things bought you went to Imschweiler's for ice cream. For ten cents they gave you so much ice cream that you could hardly eat it all. And they gave you a plate of salty pretzels free. If you wanted steam pretzels, the kind with soft parts, they charged a penny apiece for them.

Imschweiler's had candy for sale too, but the best candy was across the main street at Golamis' Sweet Shop. They made a molasses twist candy that had a coconut cream filling; no one has ever made anything like that since.

It cost 35 cents to go to Mauch Chunk, but the 35-mile ride was worth it. This is the place where the prisoner in Mollie Maguire times had put his hand on the cell wall and said: "If I am guilty, this handprint will fade away, but if I am innocent, it will stay forever." They hanged the man, but the handprint never went away. You could see it on the walls of the old jail. Besides using trolleys you could go on the Switchback Railroad.

The Switchback Railroad started right in the town. The brakeman on the cars let go the brakes, and the train of cars rolled by gravity to the foot of a plane railroad. Here a little tow car caught hold of the train and great hauling engines pulled it up to the top of a mountain. The train coasted down by gravity to the foot of another mountain, and again a plane engine hauled the cars to the top. After coasting into the town of Summit Hill, the train stopped while everyone got out and walked around and had lunch. There were stores that sold things made of anthracite coal—paper weights, little pyramids with thermometers on them, and ashtrays. There were rings with sulphur diamonds set in them. The names of the plane mountains were Mt. Jefferson and Mt. Pisgah.

You got back on the cars; the breakman pushed them to get started and then hopped aboard. You raced all the way back to Mauch Chunk by gravity. You were almost a thousand feet above sea level at Summit Hill, and you came down almost the full thousand feet in one great rush. On the last straight stretch the cars must have gone a mile a minute! That was the world's biggest roller coaster.

From Mauch Chunk you took a Lehigh Valley train and went about five miles to Glen Onoko Park. There you could climb on ladders and stairways following Onoko Creek's cascade to the top of the mountain at Packer's Point.

On a clear night they said that you could see the lights of New York City more than a hundred miles away. In the daytime you could see the Delaware Water Gap and three states—Pennsylvania, New Jersey, and New York.

It was possible to go from Minersville to New York by trolley car. You went to Pottsville and then on to Reading. From there the trolley took you to Allentown, Bethlehem, and Easton and across the Delaware River into New Jersey. It took most all day to make the trip, but it could be done, and it was a real trolley car adventure.

Whenever we went to Brooklyn, New York, to see my grandparents, we went by train. It was wonderful to go by train, especially if my father was with us. He knew all the engineers and conductors and brakemen on the Philadelphia & Reading trains. And he would stand by the telegrapher's office in the station and tell you what those mysterious noises on the telegraph sounder meant. He would read off the messages and the numbers on the coal cars that were being hauled to Philadelphia. Once upon a time he himself had been a telegraph operator away out in Missouri on the Missouri Pacific Railroad. He used to tell me about it. His telegraph office was at a railroad junction near a big swamp, and he never heard anything except bullfrogs all the time he was out there. He said he found out that the bullfrogs could talk, and he used to talk bullfrog to me. But I couldn't understand it.

We never bought the regular kind of tickets when we traveled by train. We used what they called a mileage book. The book had a thousand little yellow tickets in it, each one good for one mile of travel. The conductor would tear off one ticket for each person for each mile traveled. The books cost $20 each.

We took the P & R train to Schuylkill Haven and got off there to wait for the flyer to come south from Pottsville. The train to Schuylkill Haven was a local and had a couple of passenger cars and a baggage car on it. But the express from Pottsville had parlor cars on it, besides lots of passenger coaches. We didn't take a parlor car, because we were only going as far as Reading on the P & R.

At Reading we changed and got the Lehigh Valley's Queen of the Valley Eastbound. This was a crack express train that came from Harrisburg. This took us to Jersey City. There we walked across the street from the depot and boarded the Liberty Street Ferry for New York.

The ferry boat had paddle wheels and a great engine that was regulated by a big "walking beam" atop the center of the ferry. You could walk along the center of the ferry and watch the great shining pistons and gears driving the paddle wheels. There was an accordian player on the ferry and little boys who shined shoes. The ride to New York cost five cents. On the way you could see the Statue of Liberty and Ellis Island, where the immigrants came in from the old country.

When the ferry boat reached the New York ferry slip, your heart was in your mouth. You were sure that the ferry would miss the slip, or that it would be going so fast it would get wrecked. But the ferry boat captain brought the ferry in slick as a whistle, the sides scraping the worn, greenish brown piles and sort of nudging them so the piles gave way a little. Then the ferry would stop right in place. There would be a rattle of chains, and the hands would let down the landing ramp for the horses and people to go ashore.

We took one crosstown trolley to the end of the Brooklyn Bridge and another to Fulton Street in Brooklyn. We crossed the Brooklyn Bridge. It was longer than the Tumbling Run bridge, but I don't think it was higher.

And then it was "Franklin Street", and we got off and walked a little piece to where my grandparents lived.

It was a wonderful trip.

Pies Are for Eating

The bright sun peeped over the knife-straight summit of Sharp Mountain in a sky as blue as a mountain lake. It would be a perfect July day.

In the hearts of a couple dozen kids—mine among them —it was certain that a good God had answered our prayers. It would be THE day for the Sunday School picnic.

Shined and dressed—unfortunately—in near Sunday best pants, shirts, dresses, we were pestering to get going before it was eight o'clock. But mothers held us all in leash for another hour or so. Finally we set out—on foot, of course— for the woods we called The Pioneers.

You walked out Third Street to the mining patch we called Schaeffer's Hill. There a little used woods road took off through a tangle of laurel into the beginnings of the tall pines that gave the grove its name. No mine woodsman's axe had yet touched these lordly trees, true pioneers of the time when only trappers and Indian hunting parties roamed the hills and valleys, long before Nicho Allen had found that black stones burned hot and bright.

We all hushed as we entered the shadows of the grove. Only the sounds of a little breeze whispering through the pine-tree tops broke the silence.

It was about a quarter of a mile until we came to the glade in the middle of the grove where picnics were held. The ground was covered with pine needles—a deep, soft, warm brown carpet that smelled so of the pines themselves.

Early as we were, we found that some of the men of the Sunday School—Will Kantner, George Geanslen, Wood Felix, Harry Laudeman, Joe Levan—were already there.

They were busy setting up boards laid on sawhorses for picnic tables. Long sheets of wrapping paper were stretched on the boards as tablecloths. In the stone fireplace that had served countless picnickers, a fire was burning bright and big coffee pots were ready, filled with water from the cold spring a hundred feet away in a laurel thicket.

Big wooden tubs filled with ice awaited the squeezing of lemons and the addition of sugar to be filled with the most delicious lemonade.

In the shadows of the laurel stood big green painted wooden tubs about three feet high, each with its tin container of ice cream—vanilla, chocolate, strawberry—packed in a brine of rock salt and cracked ice.

Wood Felix—a huge man with twinkling eyes and a prodigious appetite—sliced delicately thin slices of heavenly pink boiled ham and piled it on plates. Already he had mountains of cheese ready—covered by clean white cheesecloth to ward against the few flies that penetrated the resin-smelling woods.

The women of the English Lutheran Church busied themselves setting out the table. Every family brought more food to the growing store. There were hard-boiled eggs, peeled and pickled in a mixture of beet juice and vinegar—bright red they were with a tangy taste of the vinegar. Chow-chow, potato salad, schmierkäse, apple butter, jams, jellies, fresh baked bread, roll butter, lettuce wilted under a hot mixture of vinegar and diced crisp bacon, pepper cabbage, pickles, shoofly and fruit and berry pies, cookies and cake.

As for cakes: to us kids cakes were cakes, to be eaten as soon as possible after a solid stuffing of the other oddments on the table. But to the knowing women of the congregation, cakes were a matter of immediate personal concern, inspection, and comment. Mrs Ruller would be sure to bring her masterpiece—a three-layer coconut cake. Mrs. Kraus specialized in devil's food—that deep red-brown chocolate cake with a butter soft icing. Mrs. Laubenstein contributed one of her celebrated pound cakes. All met with critical nods, lavish praise, and deprecating smiles from the various bakers.

As I say, to us kids, cakes were cakes. So we never heard the little whispers, "Which one is Mrs. Huntzinger's?" That was one cake invariably reserved by common consent for us shavers. Mrs. Huntzinger, to put it delicately, was not noted for the cleanliness of her kitchen.

Not that anything distressingly untoward had ever been discovered in her cakes. Oh, there may have been a frieze of cat hairs protruding from one of the iced layers. And there were rumors that bits of rags from a dustcloth and even a small feather or so from a chicken-plucking moment had been encountered. But nothing much. Only just enough to make certain that we youngsters got the cake, the whole cake and whatever might be in it, edible or inedible.

It was superb cake. Three huge, fluffy layers. Rich, rich chocolate with thick, thick buttery creamy icing between layers and on top and sides. And bits of canned red cherries dotting the top like little red islands in a frothy sea. That Mrs. Huntzinger was berating fate for the loss of something or other around her kitchen didn't stop young jaws from working sturdily at the pleasant task of demolishing Mrs. Huntzinger's beautiful though damned cake. It wasn't until little Tommy Richards, munching happily on a huge piece, came up with an, "Ow! I broke me toot'!" that anyone paid heed to Mrs. Huntzinger's mutterings. Tommy reached into his icing-chocolate ringed mouth and came up with his "toot" and a tiny bell!

"Ach Gott" cried Mrs. Huntzinger happily. "Mine pussy's bell to keep her from eatin' the little birds yet. Now I know where it went, danks be to Gott."

Well, Tommy's "toot" was only a baby tooth that was due to come out soon anyway, so no harm was done. But it all added to Mrs. Huntzinger's hard-won reputation as a careless baker.

Not all was cake when it came to desserts on the long picnic table. There were pies.

And, there being pies, there naturally was a pie-eating contest.

Huckleberries being well in season, the pie to be eaten by the contestants would, of course, be one of those luscious, dark blue, oh-so-juicy huckleberry pies.

Our English Lutheran Sunday School had a champion of champions. Round the Sunday School picnic circuit he circulated, gulping down pies with the utmost abandon, the ultimate speed, and the minimum of mess. We knew him affectionately as "Goozer" Starr.

Now how he got the name "Goozer" is a secret of the past—his past, to be sure. There were those who said it came from the first pie-eating contest he entered wherein the subject of the contest was gooseberry pie. This is quite unlikely as nobody ever made pies of gooseberries, at least in our circle of pie makers. There were those that said the nickname may have come from the attempt of the pie-eater to say "Juicy" with a mouthful of pie unswallowed. At any rate, "Goozer" it was, and "Goozer" was our champion.

The pie-eating contest was the high point of the planned activities of the picnic, which included three-legged races, potato sack races, egg-on-spoon races, hop, step, and jump competitions, hoop rolling for the girls.

There was most definitely a winning technique in eating a pie without use of hands, feet, fork, spoon or any gnawing device except a set of strong teeth. First—the pie. That was one-half of a generous ten-inch-diameter huckleberry pie oozing with dark blue juices, pretty enough to warrant a picture, tempting enough to make the mouth water. The pie was on a tin plate. The contestants were lined up on the picnic table benches, hands tied behind their backs. The pie was on a level with their respective mouths. At the word "GO!" a dozen young heads dove for the pies, a dozen mouths opened, a dozen sets of teeth tried for a bite at the slippery pie and the contest was desperately on.

The pie dishes slithered. The more the blueberry juice splashed on the table, the more the plates slipped around. The more desperate the attempts to stop the slipping, the more blue juice on face, in hair, on mouth. Sometimes the pie, taking on a distinct will of its own, would slither right off into the contestant's lap. That disqualified him and brought him face to face with his mother, armed with a wet rag.

But "Goozer", our champion, had a technique of his own. Before the word "GO!" had crackled in his ear, he had studied the situation as a born sportsman would. He calculated thickness of crust, depth of filling, quantity of juice— and his field of foes.

His operation was uniquely simple. At the starting word his chin went forward until it was almost over the cut edge of the pie. Then it went down with a crack, holding the plate firmly on the table. Automatically his jaws went to work, chomping away in great bites of the pie. As his teeth progressed into the juicy mess his chin kept pace, taking new grip on the tin plate as the pie disappeared. All through the soft center of the pie this human shovel drove, licking the last bits of juice from the shell of the pie still left on the edges of the plate. With a final swirl of his head and chin, "Goozer" would revolve the pie plate, grab the remaining crust in his teeth and gobble it for all the world like a robin gulping a worm.

"Goozer" always won. For all I know, he may still be eating pies—enjoying them—setting new records. I hope so.

What did he win this time? A genuine 25 cent League Slugger bat!

The picnic tables were "redded up" after the pie eating contest, and then there was a baseball game between the boys and the girls, but that wasn't much fun because the girls got five strikes and the boys had to hit left handed. But we won anyway. The prize was only a few peanuts apiece, but they were fair won and tasted the better.

There was a great pole swing in the pine grove. Only the bigger boys were allowed to swing on it. In fact they were the only ones who dared try it.

In the long ago someone had driven a long iron bar, about an inch in diameter, through the trunks of two tall pine trees. From this bar two oak saplings, maybe two to three inches thick, were wired to iron collars that were clamped around the bar. At the bottom of the saplings, which were about 15 feet long, there was a wooden slat for a footstand. You stood on this slat and began to swing. The most daring of the big boys could ride the swing until it was almost horizontal with the ground. Then they would swoosh down and up until they were parallel with the ground again. The pole swing was practically guaranteed to provide a few choice bruises, and, not occasionally, a broken arm, collarbone, or leg.

There was a smaller swing for us little tads. But we looked longingly at the big one and hoped for THE DAY.

Of course not all the bounteous food supply had been consumed at noon time. There was plenty to eat in the late afternoon—a fresh batch of lemonade was made to drink. Then, with every little belly and every big stomach loaded, and the sun beginning to fade, we all walked slowly to what we fondly called "the brow of the hill." Far below we could see our town. We looked hard to spot our own homes, sitting like little doll houses in the distance. A little to the right the sun was going down in a tremendous aura of color.

Our English Lutheran preacher was a big man, really big, but he was kind and gentle. His name was Forscht, and he

s. gilman

The Pole Swing at the Pioneers

came from somewhere north of the Broad Mountain. He had offered grace at the noon meal and the evening meal. Now as we all sat on the grass covered hilltop he once more asked God's mercy on all of us.

Then he began to sing, very softly, and we all joined in:

"Abide with me, fast falls the eventide,
    The darkness deepens, Lord with me abide;
When other help has failed to comfort me,
    Help of the helpless, oh abide with me."

Two Wheels Are Better Than Four

Mr. Lou Roehrig sold wallpaper, window shades, picture frames and the like in our town. He was a little man, his head bald on top, with a tiny fringe all around the edges of the bald spot. He had a round little belly and laughed a lot, and I always thought that he could fill in for Santa Claus if Santa was sick some Christmastime. Of course he would have had to wear a false beard.

My mother sent me to Mr. Roehrig's store one day. It was hot and sticky, and it sort of felt like a thunderstorm was making. It was sometime in early August. It can get awful hot in the mountains of eastern Pennsylvania in August. It made you think that it would be swell to swim in Long Dam. But Long Dam was about a mile walk; it was too hot to walk that far. Now if you had a bicycle. . .

It was sort of cool in Mr. Roehrig's store. I looked around and cooled off a bit. Mr. Roehrig was making a picture frame out of wood that had gold paint on it. I watched him working, and it looked like a pretty good job to me. I forget what I was sent over to Mr. Roehrig's store for. At any rate, I never got it. For Mr. Roehrig looked at me sort of funny-like, smiled, and said, right out of the clear blue sky, "William, how would you like a bicycle?"

That was like asking a small boy how he would like to be turned loose in a candy store with a scoop shovel. Or like giving the cashier in a bank a satchel and telling him to help himself.

My mouth opened wide enough to catch butterflies.

"A bicycle!" I faltered.

"You don't have one, do you?" Mr. Roehrig asked.

Speechless, I shook my head.

"Well, now you run over to the postoffice and ask your father if you can have my bike."

It was a hundred yards from Mr. Roehrig's store to the postoffice where my father was the postmaster. This is the first time in recorded history that the hundred yard dash was made in under ten seconds.

My heels smoked as I took the three steps up to the postoffice in the Opera House.

I pounded on the door marked "POSTMASTER." Miss Emmie Higley, the assistant postmistress, looked out the Stamp Window in panic. Miss Bess Robinson poked her head out the Money Order Window, sure there was a catastrophe. My father opened the door. All I could get out were words like: "Mr. Roehrig . . . Bike . . . Me . . . Can I . . .?"

My father said, "Whoa now, William! Hold your hosses! Calm down!"

I blurted out the details of the most amazing offer ever made to anyone anywhere.

"Now that's right neighborly of Lou," he said. "Of course you may have the bike. You go back and tell him I said it was all right. And be sure to tell him how happy you are to get it and thank him."

Mr. Roehrig took me back of his store to his loft where he kept all his picture framing wood and his window shades. He pulled an old sheet off a shapeless form. There it was! It was a Columbia; it was the most beautiful bike in the whole world. It had nickel handle bars. It had a tool bag with wrenches and such. It needed paint, after the years of storage, and the tires were flat. But it was beautiful. And it was mine!

I stuttered my thanks. I remembered to tell him how happy I was.

Then he said, solemnly, "William, I got to warn you . . ." my heart stood still, "I got to warn you that this was a hard luck bike. I hope it won't be for you. I got it to go on a Century Run. I wasn't more than ten miles on that grind when I hit a rock, updumped the bike and broke my leg. I never rode it after that. Now do you still want it?"

Did I want it? Seven teams of horses couldn't have torn my sweaty fingers away from that bicycle.

I painted my bike black with red trimmings. My father bought me two new tires, some tire patches, a bell, and a carbide lamp that clamped on the front post. You could light it at night, and it was bright as day ahead. And you could take the lamp off and use it when you fished at night or went frog hunting. Coaster brakes hadn't been invented. When I wanted to slow down or stop, I put my foot on the front tire and "spragged" it—coal town language for braking.

I was forever free of utilities and big corporations. No longer need I pay a nickel to go to Pottsville on the trolley. No longer need I pay eight cents to ride the miner train to Pine Knot, nor a nickel to get to Indian Run. I could take my bike. If I wanted to go to Long Dam to swim in the muddy water, I could take my own time and ride my bike. If Gyp got tired trotting alongside, I could hold him in my lap with one hand and steer with the other. He didn't like riding a bike as well as riding on the cowcatcher on the old Cannonball locomotive from the Indian Run water tank to town.

I don't know how many miles I rode on that bicycle. It was the only one I ever owned. I know that every mile was a delight. And I never fell off, never hurt myself.

About this time I had my first ride in an automobile— which we called an automoBEEL. My cousin Charlie had a Maxwell. My Uncle Al had a Rambler when Ramblers were huge, luxurious cars. Our next door neighbor, Sam Crawford, had a fire-engine red Thomas, with seats in the tonneau that climbed heavenward and were upholstered in genuine red leather. John and Morgan Lewis, who ran the knitting mill, had a Locomobile.

The Locomobile was a ponderous car. All us kids used to gather around and watch Mr. John or Mr. Morgan polish the brasswork, fill the lamps with carbide and water, polish the body, put neatsfoot oil on the cloth top. Then we would watch in awe as one of the brothers would wind the crank on the side. When the engine would roar to life the older brother would shift the gears, and off they would go.

None of us had ever had a ride in an automobile. That was one of those unlikely dream-type things in the back of our heads.

This Saturday afternoon we were getting in the way of Mr. John and Mr. Morgan—Charlie Wernert, Clint Mervine, Georgie Phillips were there with me.

The big Locomobile was shined to a mirror. Suddenly Mr. John said, "How would you boys like to go for a ride?"

We were pop-eyed. He opened the tonneau door for us and we crept carefully in, sitting on the edge of the rich leather seats. Mr. Morgan cranked the engine; it took hold with an earth shattering rumble. He clambered up on the big front seat beside his brother. Mr. John put the car in gear, and we were off.

It was wonderful. There we were going faster than fast, down Carbon Street, down Delaware Avenue, across Sunbury Street, on the Upper Road toward Pottsville. We saw people we knew. We waved. They waved wonderingly back. Mr. John sounded the big horn by pressing the rubber ball at the end of it.

It wasn't any time until we were in Yorkville and heading down Market Street to downtown Pottsville. With a grand flourish Mr. John pulled to the curb in front of Imschweiler's Ice Cream Parlor. "All right, boys, what say to some ice cream?"

An auto ride AND free ice cream! How lordly can you feel?

We came out to the car again well filled by a big ten-cent plate of ice cream (I had chocolate) and pretzels.

The sky was a peculiar shade of bronze. In the distance there was a rumble of thunder. Mr. Morgan looked up and then said, "Hop in boys, we'll beat that storm home!"

They headed north to take the Bullshead Road back. It was a hilly road, not as good as the main road out of the county seat, but it had little road traffic. The clouds grew heavier and lightning flashed. We kept looking over our shoulders as the storm clouds spread. Mr. John laughed and fed more gas to the big car. It roared up the hills and flashed down the hills. The storm was racing with us. As we came to the top of the last hill before we were in town, the first drops of rain began to fall.

Now the lightning flashes streaked all across the sky. Great jagged bolts slammed earthward. The thunder was continuous. Right in back of us we could see the curtain of rain hitting the dusty road. Over the brow of the hill we

S. gilman

roared. Then down, down, down the mile-long grade. Mr. John fed more gasoline to the pounding engine. Nearer came the sheet of rain. Louder came the thunder-claps. Brighter came the lightning, now almost crimson in color. Mr. John gave never a thought to the main line of the railroad at the foot of the hill. He roared the car across the tracks. We kids bounced up from our seat and, I swear, didn't come down until we were stopped in front of our house on Carbon Street. "Run, boys!" Mr. Morgan yelled. We ran on our porch. The clouds burst and sheets of rain almost hid the big Locomobile from view.

I'll never forget that ride. When I told my father about it, he said "That man's a fool. Any man who drives one of those automobeels is a fool. Don't you ever go out with those Lewises again." I never did, of course, but I did go for rides with my cousin and my uncle. But they never raced a storm four miles—and won.

The Night the Snow Burned

A pair of zesty brothers, John and Edward Biddle by name, perpetrated a murder in western Pennsylvania, were caught, tried, and found guilty. Lodged in the Allegheny County Jail awaiting the gallows, John found a soft spot in the tender heart of the comely wife of the warden, Mrs. Peter Stoffel. She came up with an escape plan for her new sweetheart and his brother. The eve of January 30, 1902 was the time set for the break. In a blinding snowstorm, with the help of a rope ladder furnished by Mrs. Stoffel, the two murderers went over the stone wall. The love-stricken Mrs. Stoffel had a sleigh waiting and lashed the horses in a wild flight through the night. The law caught up with them. The Biddle boys were slain, and Mrs. Stoffel got a bullet in her breast.

This drama in real life was immortalized in "A Break for Liberty, or The Biddle Boys Dash for Life," and in due time a wandering troupe of players brought the melodrama to our Opera House. On the bill for the week's engagement for these thespians was "Uncle Tom's Cabin," "Way Down East," and "East Lynn." But the townsfolk were waiting for the Biddle play, since it was fresh in the news.

Our Opera House was the largest building in town—three stories high. It housed the postoffice on the first floor front and the auditorium occupied the two floors above. No Opera, as such, ever played the House, but it was host to wandering minstrel troupes, "Tom" shows, basketball games, and graduation exercises for the High School. Dances were held there in winter. While they were not to be compared with the Pottsville Assembly (nobody from Minersville except the veriest Quality Hill snobs went to THAT), the dances did attract the town's most eligible bachelors and most fetching maidens.

Set up for the visit of the Biddle company, the Opera House boasted 150 seats on the floor and 50 or so backless wooden benches in the "peanut gallery" in the rear.

A gaudy curtain, executed by one of our town's budding artists, concealed the stage before the performance began. This was a moneymaker for the Opera House, for there were rented panels, done in richly appropriate colors, advertising the wares of various of the town merchants. "When Oysters 'R' In Season See John Reiss," said one. "You Furnish the Girl, We'll Furnish the Ring" proudly boasted Mortimer's Jewelry store. "Time is Our Main Object" said the Joseph Gerz, Watchmaker, sign. A soulful looking steer peered at the audience from the sign that said "George Barrett, Finest of Fresh and Smoked Meats. Try us, you'll go nowhere else." "Undertaking in all its Branches, also Fine Furniture" was the offering of Mr. Weiser, the town mortician—a word that hadn't been invented yet. "Feed, Food, and Flour—Any Quantities Promptly Delivered," said Franz Kraus, local miller. "Electricity Neatly Done," was cryptically messaged by F. R. Schneider, the town's first electrician.

The Opera House had a props man. He was also the janitor, the watchman, the sound effects man and general jack of all trades around the theater and was available for any and all odd jobs in his spare time. Long, hot summer days would find him seated in a dilapidated wicker chair alongside the remains of a Civil War mortar, at the "Stage Door" on Third Street. His was the job of setting out the seats for drama, of fastening hoops for basketball games, of coating the floor with coarse-ground cornmeal for dancing. This made the floor somewhat slippery, but didn't do much for the splinters in the old pine. The glide of the schottische was likely to end abruptly with a muttered prevarication on the part of the male partner in a dance.

The props man was Tommy Jones. He was a stocky gnome of a man always ready to gossip. He smoked what was without doubt the oldest, smelliest pipe in town. It was always alight, always smoking like a badly trimmed lamp wick. He was partial to "Miner's Extra," which was made up of one third tobacco stems, one third tobacco waste, and one third leaves, hay, or other burnable rubbish. It was real powerful.

Tommy could be relied upon to produce the jingling of sleighbells (real), the roar of thunder (the rattling of a sheet of tin), the neighing of a horse (personally produced), the blast of an explosion (a smart blow on a bass drum), the falling of rain (rice grains vigorously shaken in a tin pan) and the snows of a blizzard.

Having been well briefed by the manager of the company on the Biddle Boys script, Tommy realized that his very best efforts would be called on this night, for the daring escape from prison was carried out in a howling blizzard through which the heroine herself drove the sleigh.

Tommy was a busy man that afternoon. From far and near he gathered great quantities of the Minersville *Free Press,* our weekly newspaper, thus cheating many of our food, fish, and meat purveyors of needed wrapping paper. Tommy cut, tore, slashed, and shredded these copies of the local voice of freedom (Ira Jones, no relation to Tommy, Proprietor and Editor) into a mountain of tiny bits of white, —or at least gray-white "snow." This he packed into burlap bags and hauled up into the flies of the theater, with sundry other props, such as the sleighbells. Then he rested on his laurels with the aid of free lunch at Gallo's saloon and a few schooners of Yuengling's very excellent beer and awaited the moment to hoist the curtain (another of Tommy's jobs).

As the climax of the drama neared, Tommy posted himself in the flies and started to drop his snow. It was most artistic. The flakes fell gently at the start, befitting the dead quiet of the night. Tommy jingled the sleighbells softly. Then he let the snow come down more heavily. With one hand he threw his snow, with the other he jingled the bells, louder and louder, to signify the oncoming sleigh. In the wings Joe Duffy, hired at the price of two beers, waved a huge fan that set the snow to swirling. Tommy was working at full speed. One hand for the bells, one hand for the snow. Now he stopped ringing the bells and threw down double handsful of snow as the heroine dashed on stage. The snow fell in blinding gusts. Duffy waved his fan frantically.

There was one small error. Tommy, as usual, had his pipe stoked up and roaring. The tobacco was red hot, the snow came down in blankets. Tommy leaned enthusiastically to his task. The blazing dottle from the pipe fell like a small red comet. The heroine waved the rope ladder she had brought for the rescue over the prison walls. She opened her mouth to speak her lines. But she stood gaping as the "snow" began to smoke, then burst into flame. "My God!" she screamed, completely forgetting the script, "The goddam snow's afire! Help! Help! Help!"

Some hero grabbed a firebucket. Luckily it was filled—something of a minor miracle—and sloshed it in the general direction of the blaze. Most of it caught the heroine full in the face. "You crazy galoot!" she shouted. "Put the fire out, not me!"

Someone dashed out and ran to the Mountaineer Fire Company up Third Street. As there were no paid firemen, this was a futile errand. By the time runners had gone to various saloons to scare up men to pull the hose cart, the fire was over. The play resumed, with the snow pretty well "melted."

My father was with me in the "peanut gallery." He said the fire was by far the best part of the show. I thought the whole show was pretty good. It cost ten cents a seat to go to the Opera House when we sat in the "peanut gallery."

When the Bijou Dream opened, the Opera House began to lose business. Not many people wanted to see the old melodramas when the new movies could be seen for only a nickel. Will Jones and Will Kantner, two of Minersville's better business men, opened the Bijou Dream in a store on Sunbury Street. The store had been vacant for a long time. The English Lutheran Church used to have its sauerkraut suppers there in the fall. And when there was an election the room was used for election rallies after torchlight parades.

The seats for the movies were just chairs that Jones and Kantner rented in town from Mr. Weiser, the Protestant undertaker and from Mr. Hummell, the Catholic undertaker. Even in death, you see, there was a division over who would get the bodies, if not the souls of the dead. The undertaking business was pretty well split along religious lines. Even when it came to renting chairs.

The room was long and narrow, and the seats were placed in rows with the sole passageway on the left hand side of the room facing the white movie screen. The projection booth was in a little box affair that the operator reached by a wooden ladder. The projector was lighted by arc-lights and was operated by a hand crank. A reel of film rolled for maybe ten to fifteen minutes, followed by a sign flashed on the screen "One Minute While We Change Reels." Advertising signs were shown before the show, along with hints on etiquette, such as "Ladies Will Remove Their Hats, All Others Must Do So," "Positively No Smoking! This Means You," "No Whistling or Stamping of Feet While Picture is Being Shown."

An illustrated song preceded the movie. The words to the song were on slides which had colored pictures to illustrate the song. Marie Kantner played and Pauline sang. The audience joined in the chorus.

It wasn't long before the Opera House succumbed and began showing movies too. Then there were no more 10-20-

30 cent melodramas. I often wondered what happened to the Biddle Boys and their nearly-incinerated heroine sweetheart; Little Eva and Topsy and Uncle Tom and Simon Legree; the wicked old man who threw his daughter out into the snow in "Way Down East: "Go, girl, Go! You are no longer daughter of mine! Go!" "Oh father! father! How can you be so cruel as to send me out into the cold snowy night?" And what ever became of Jack Dalton, USA, and his stirring curtain to the question: "And who are you, sir?" "I am Jack Dalton, USA."

In Pottsville, the Academy of Music, boasting a larger theater, kept melodrama, vaudeville, and minstrels alive for a longer time. My favorite magician was Allan Keller— "Keller the Great"—and his partner and magic heir Howard Thurston. But it cost money to go in to Pottsville and more to get into the theater, so we didn't go over there very often. Besides you got a real bargain in the movies for five cents. Pearl White in "The Perils of Pauline," Mr. and Mrs. Sidney Drew, John Bunny and Flora Finch, Blanche Sweet, Mae Marsh, Lillian and Dorothy Gish, Mary Pickford, Anita Stewart, Elsie Ferguson, William and Dustin Farnum, Noah and Wallace Beery, Slim Summerville, Chester Conklin, Ambrose Swain, Ben Turpin, Charlie Chaplin.

There were big lenses in the movie projector which quite frequently broke under the intense heat of the arc-lamps. Then, if you were lucky, you might get a piece. The lenses were about four inches in diameter and almost an inch thick. Even a small piece made a good burning glass. You could burn holes in pieces of paper and even set it on fire.

When we went over to John James' farm, in the woods there, to cook the eggs and potatoes we had "annexed" at Rube Geist's Lytle farm, we could start our fire with the burning glass. This was better than rubbing sticks together, or whatever the Indians used to do.

And there was always a chance when we went over to James' woods that there might have been a beer picnic the day before, and the brewery wagon drivers would be over picking up the empty kegs. While the picnic was on, the picnickers used to roll the barrels down hill into the little stream at the bottom where we always cooked our eggs and things. The beer wagon drivers were too lazy to come down to get these kegs, so we used to roll them up hill, and the drivers paid us five cents for a 'sexile' as we called the small one (sixth barrel) and ten cents—princely sum—for half barrels.

The burning glass would bring money back to the Bijou Dream, that way.

A Tin Cup of Bean Soup

No days flew faster than the last days of summer. No steps lagged more than those we took on the way to visit Doc Andrews.

Doc Andrews may have been just as kind as Doc Kistler. His affection for his patients probably was just as great. But the trouble was, we only went to Doc Andrews when our teeth hurt.

I suppose corrective dentistry, braces, visit-your-dentist-every-six-months and all that had already been invented in the big cities. But nothing of this regimen had penetrated the coal region. "I got a toothache!" was the last anguished word before the visit to Doc Andrews' office.

His office was in what would have been the parlor, or front room, of his home on Quality Hill. Now Doc Andrews lived at the bottom of the Hill. His place thus was not quite a part of the hill on which dwelt the gentry of the town. However, while his business was but tolerated, he and his family were accepted by other Quality Hillers.

When you walked into his office you immediately saw the place where you were about to suffer. The dental chair was of red plush with a fringe of long gold tassels about the seat. The back tilted, somewhat like a barber's chair, and there was a headrest. The dental "engine" was foot powered, and the drills revolved about ten times a minute—or so it seemed to the patient. The good Doc kept up the usual running river of conversation—even as do dentists today—while he drilled and picked and packed away. Was a tooth to come out—it came, without too much benefit of anesthetics. But he was a good dentist.

His worst customer was one Francis Andrews. Now Francis was never known by any other name than "Monk," for reasons unknown to me. I do know that "Monk" could spit through his front teeth, an accomplishment admired by all of us kids. And the reason why he could do this was because he had a perfect hole in between his two front teeth. Through this he could direct his saliva with deadly precision. Doc Andrews could never persuade his son "Monk" to sit in his dental chair. "Monk" would have lost face—had he done so. So the "spittin' " hole stayed, Doc shook his head and "Monk" spit away happily.

Late in August the circus came to our town. It wasn't like the giant ones that played at Dolan's Park—Sells-Floto, or Barnum & Bailey, or Buffalo Bill's Wild West. We took the trolley to Railway Park for these circuses and walked up the hill to Yorkville to Dolan's Park, which was only a big flat clayey field.

The one circus that came to our town that I remember was Col. Conlon's Great Dog and Pony Show. It wasn't a great canvas like the big shows, but they had a tent, a sideshow, and a menagerie, just like the big shows.

Now there were two places in our town a circus could pitch its tents. One rented for $5 a day, and the other cost $15 a day. There was a very great difference, but only the natives knew it. The circus people didn't. Some people like Col. Conlon went for the $5 dollar place, which I guess was all he could afford.

All of us kids pitched in to get the circus set up in this field, which was right alongside the coaldirt-black West Branch. We lugged stakes, hauled on ropes, ran errands, and generally got in the way. Of course the man with the free tickets never did show up after the work was done. The first performance was set for seven o'clock that evening. About five o'clock great black clouds rushed down from the mountain valleys. Thunder roared. Rain came down in buckets. The reason for the $5 rental soon was distressingly learned by the circus people. The West Branch became a raging torrent within minutes. The black waters swept over the circus. Seats collapsed, stakes loosened, the main tent collapsed. Circus people—girls and men—fought terrified ponies to the one spot of high ground in the field. But the menagerie—with it a cage of snakes—took off for Reading and points south.

Clint Mervine and I went snake hunting next day. We figured if we had one, we could start our own circus. Somewhere I read how you could put a loop of rawhide across a forked stick and catch a snake with it. We made one up and went looking along the black banks of the river, now back in its course again. We clumped in the mud, getting gloriously dirty, poked gingerly into bushes. About a mile down stream we found one. But he didn't like the sulfur water and was very dead. We brought him back to our house, but my mother made me throw him on the town dump. The Col. Conlon Great Dog and Pony Show never came back. Others did, though. Most took the $15 field, which was dry at flood time.

We knew that summer was about over when the Grand Army veterans held their annual bean soup gala over at Furnace Grove.

Furnace Grove was not too far from the railroad depot. It was a place of tall maples, oaks, chestnuts. There was a tiny pond where the fishing for sunfish and catfish was fair to middling. In the winter it was one of our favorite skating spots.

In the Grove, in the distant past, the Veterans had erected a dance floor and had built wooden platforms for tents and stone fireplaces on which the bean soup would be cooked in great iron kettles. Navy beans were soaked overnight, put in the kettles with ham bones, and simmered for hours. My Uncle Joe Levan—one of the brighter elements in the GAR ranks—was boss of the cooking. His experience dated back to his cook's duties in the Civil War. He had a secret blend of herbs, spices, salt and pepper that he mixed himself, bagged, and poured some into each bubbling kettle. Whatever the seasoning was, his bean soup "Wilderness Style" was as tasty as bean soup ever can get. There was coffee or lemonade to wash it down. You got a big tin mug of bean soup, a big hunk of home baked bread, and a mug of hot steaming coffee—or cold lemonade if you were a kid—for 25 cents. The profits went to the GAR post. Since the beans, ham, coffee and lemonade were donated by friends of the Veterans, it was pretty well all profit. My Uncle Joe always gave me a lot of beans in my mug of soup and never seemed to see the quarter I proffered. This made him my friend for life—and made me the envy of hungry friends. The GAR men had real army tents on wooden platforms, and you could go in a tent and see how they lived when they were fighting the Rebels. They had their rifles, and cartridge belts, and campaign uniforms in the tents.

There was dancing on the big wooden platform, too. All the people danced waltzes, schottisches, two steps, and reels. I didn't dance—but that was because I couldn't.

Children find life is full of pitfalls, of consummate evils, of disappointments, of plots by their elders to encompass their downfall.

I had scarcely realized that I could not dance when, one horrible autumn day after school, I was told that that night I would be expected to present myself at dancing school.

I had heard some rumors about this school but had tossed them blithely off as just parent talk. It was unthinkable that my cousin Mabel from Ashland, across the Broad Mountain, would come all the way down to our town to torture me weekly. But that is the way it was. Cousin Mabel, with Cousin Ray by her side to provide the music, was going to open a dancing school in our town. It would be at Mine Workers Hall on Third Street.

Mine Workers Hall was just what the name implied—a hall where our hard-bitten coal miners gathered to discuss their quarrels with the company, listen to their union leaders, and decide whether to strike or not. One of the queer things about these strikes, and I never knew the reason, was that they were always called in late spring or early summer when demand for anthracite coal was at its lowest point and when the mines likely would be shut down anyhow.

Well, I never was one to delve into union affairs, least of all when I was a child. I knew Mine Workers Hall, and I knew that no one could possibly dance on those floors, splintered by years of rough boots. Oh maybe the foreigners could dance there, but all they ever did was to stomp and jump and reel about to the tune of a murderously loud and unmusical band consisting of such unlikely musical combinations as a bass horn, a clarinet, a fiddle, and a drum.

My cousin Ray, of course, played none of these exotic instruments. She played the piano—and very well too, to give her full credit. My cousin Mabel had gone to dancing school in Philadelphia—she stayed with my Aunt Sue and Uncle George down there—and had several dancing schools in full blast in other coal towns in need of culture.

The torment was to begin at seven o'clock, and this would be each Thursday for the duration of eight weeks. I could see that my pre-Christmas activities would be sadly disrupted. Upcoming were such dates as Halloween, which to my dismay, fell on a Thursday. I would have to struggle along with only tick-tack night, gate night, and chalk night.

Worst of all, I had to dress up. I mean I had to put on my Sunday best suit. All my arguments—that I might fall down, that dancing was dangerous to life and limb, that I might stumble on the brick walks and ruin my best shoes, came to naught. I said that was the worst. No, the worst was that I was quickly fitted out at Mr. Kelly's shoe store with dancing pumps, silly little shoes that didn't even have laces to tie, but had *buckles* on them! Mother whipped up a bag with drawstrings to carry them in. And the only velvet she had handy was bright orange. It had to be velvet. That was the style.

I trudged slowly over to Sunbury Street, slower still to Third Street, at a crawl up the steep hill from Sunbury Street to the Hall. By the time I reached there I knew I would never be able to walk another step, let alone dance.

It was with some relief I found that I was not alone in my misery. "Scow" Zapf was there, and *his* pump bag was a violent lavender. We compared and then went into almost hysterical giggles when "Fats" Wernert arrived with a kelly green bag. "Fats" was a relative of cousins Mable and Ray, on his mother's side. As kin we two were greeted affectionately by the two girls. They kissed us!

There were girls in the school, of course. They sat on one side, we boys on the opposite side. They were eager. We were frightened fugitives from better places. They were graceful even if they didn't know a damn thing about dancing. We were all left feet and knockknees. They had rhythm, we simply stumbled out of time. It took the combined efforts of Mabel and Ray to get us even to stand up to learn the rudiments. Ray pounded the piano to instill some sense of timing into our heads.

All did not go well with our shuffling attempts to glide. The wear and tear of hobnailed miners' boots took care of that. The floor was, to put it mildly, rough. It was not only rough, but downright splintery. Dora Dietz was the first casualty when she stumbled, fell, and rammed a splinter in her shin. Laura Laudermilch tumbled too and skinned a knobby knee. My cousin Mable called me hurriedly to her rescue. She gave me a quarter and urged me to run down to Rose Bright's store—that being but three blocks away—for some cornmeal wherewith to give the floor some semblance of smoothness.

In due time, allowing for a stop to watch what appeared to be an incipient fire but which turned out to be only some rubbish being burned, I returned with a five pound sack of cornmeal. That I got it for slightly less than a quarter I didn't say, figuring the laborer was worthy of his hire. That Cousin Mable gave me a dime just added to my profits.

As provider of the cornmeal, I got the task of spreading it around. "Fats" and "Scow" helped me. I would say that a couple pounds would have done the trick. But we had the cornmeal and we used it. Well, in school we used to sing a song about the Jolly Millers, and we rated the name. All the boys got into the act, and golden cornmeal dusted everything —floor, chairs, girls, boys, piano, sheet music. Ah, it was fun. But finally we ran out of meal, quiet descended on the disaster area, and the dance lessons continued.

We did learn to dance.

Unfortunately that brought us up as fair game for "PARTIES." There were, of course, "parties" and "PARTIES." The first were those little things gotten up on the spur of the moment, with a jug of lemonade and cookies as fare. Occasions could be a birthday or just a hot day in the summer when having a party seemed the thing to do.

But a "PARTY"!

Only the grand people on Quality Hill put on a real "PARTY."

First off, you would get an invitation. This would be on fancy note paper and delivered by hand or often by mail. The invitation would state the nature of the affair. Maybe a birthday. A present was now dreamed up by parents who couldn't afford one. Since the party was on Quality Hill, the present must be the best. What to wear was of paramount importance. The boys wore their Sunday best. The girls better than their best. That meant the party would be a bore right from the start, with only the food to look forward to.

The best parties on Quality Hill were those that Marjorie

Steel gave. Marjorie was a sweet girl, always trying to be pleasing, never trying to put on airs. She was very well liked. She did live in the biggest house in Minersville, the most important one on Quality Hill, and her father was the town's biggest banker. We kids were awed by Marjorie's father. He walked ramrod stiff, his black homburg hat making him look seven feet tall. He would bow gracefully to the ladies of the town, lifting his hat clear from his head. He would bow courteously to the men of the town. He would nod graciously to the children. He was a most kind man, in fact. We always enjoyed Marjorie's parties. The Steels had a phonograph, and we could play it. There were good games with prizes. Late in the afternoon Mr. Steel would arrive, gracious as always. He would come into the great living room and ask how we were enjoying ourselves. We were, but somehow his presence sort of quieted things down. Now a little less boisterous we waited quietly for the food, which was always in great plenty. We ate, bobbed our heads to Mrs. Steel at the door and hopped for home. Another "best party" was over.

The English Lutheran Church Sauerkraut Party wound up the fall festivities. This was a supper where the main dish was sauerkraut boiled with fat pork shoulder, accompanied with all the ingredients of a picnic. Fifty cents for adults, a quarter for children and eat all you want. When this supper had come and gone you knew the year had come full cycle and Christmas wasn't far away.

When the Belsnickel Came

I never saw him, but I know there was a Santa Claus.

I never saw the Belsnickel, but I know there was one. My father saw him when he was a little boy. And he told me about him. This is what he told me:

"The Belsnickel was a horrible creature. He could be half man and half beast. He wasn't always the same. He was a bad fairy kind of monster and could take on any disguise he wanted. At one time he would come all dressed in fur; he would run in the house on all fours and make horrible growlings and snap like a mad dog. At other times he would come dressed in a Joseph's coat of all colors of patches. He'd wear an old fur cap with bells sewed to it on his head. His face could be covered with a beard and sharp pointed mustachios. And on the tails of his ragged coat and on the sleeves there would be more bells. When *that* Belsnickel came into the house he would prance around and laugh, yell, and jump at people, all the time shaking all over so the bells clattered. Sometimes Belsnickel would come like a great ghost all in a white sheet with scary white hood and great black and blood-red eyes. Oh, he was a fearful bad, bad thing!

"Belsnickel always came on Christmas Eve. And he most always came just about the time when my sister and my brother and I were hanging up our stockings. We had a fireplace in the big front parlor and there our stockings must go to be filled by Kris Kringle. There was a great scuffling and shouting, laughter and near tears as we all tried to find our biggest, longest stocking and fought for the best place—the ends of the mantle—to hang them. We were certain they would be filled to overflowing, though mother and father warned that only good boys and girls got gifts—that there

114

S. Gilman

The Belsnickel

wasn't one of us, but maybe Katie, yes, and little Jonie, that
would get a single solitary thing or maybe an onion.

"That made me feel pretty good, being 'little Jonie', the
youngest of the seven boys who made up our family, and just
a year older than sister Katie.

"Well, we were romping and quarreling away and then all of a sudden there came the most tremendous crashing knock on the kitchen door.

"We stood stunned. For a few seconds we didn't know what it was. Then the terrible thought struck us all at once. It was the Belsnickel!

"Al, he was my oldest brother, swaggered. 'I ain't scared,' he bragged. Little Katie started to cry, My mother took her in her arms and told her not to be afraid. If she was a good girl, the Belsnickel wouldn't hurt her. Nobody bothered to save *me!*

"There was another pounding at the door. A rough voice bellowed: 'Open the door. I'm looking for all the bad children in the whole wide world!'

"Mother and Father herded us into the kitchen. My father opened the door as another crashing knock and an unearthly yowl came from without.

"In came the most terrible monster we had ever seen. I yelled in terror and started to run, bumping into the table and knocking over a few assorted chairs. Big brother Al grabbed me and hung on. 'Don't let him scare you,' he quavered. But I was scared already. So was Al. And so were all the rest of us boys.

"Belsnickel was all done up in an old coat that had red and blue and crazy quilt patches all over it. There was a big belt around the coat, and he had felt miners boots on his feet. On his head there was a big old furred cap. His face was covered with a gray beard and a mustache. On his hat, on the coat sleeves, and on the tails of his coat there were little bells that rang every time he moved. On his back there was a peddlar's pack. It was knobby and rough as if there were lots of things in it. In his right hand he carried a whip.

"We children stood in a sweating tremble.

"Belsnickel's eyes glittered in the furry face. He unslung

the big pack from his back. He reached into it and grabbed a handful of candy and nuts and threw them on the floor.

" 'For the good boys and girls!' he shouted.

"Down on the floor we scrambled. This Belsnickel wasn't the ogre we had feared after all! But, ah, the trust of a little child! As our fat little bottoms stretched our pants, Belsnickel gripped his whip tight and started to flail away. The lash stung our behinds. Laughter gave way to yells of pain. Only little Katie escaped—after all she was only a baby. But the rest of us ran around the kitchen in panic trying to dodge the stinging, whistling whip. My father and mother tried to keep sober faces, but finally burst out laughing. Belsnickel, sweating, left off the whipping. He stood back and surveyed his weeping prey. 'You done things bad all year what you didn't get whopped for. Now that makes up for them times. Next year, you do bad things, you 'fess up to it, then mebbe I won't have to whop you!'

"With that he dug deep into his pack and gave us each a handful of goodies.

" 'Merry Christmas!' he shouted. He leaned over and kissed my smiling mother, shook hands with my father, and bounded out the door.

"That was Belsnickel. And it was the year of 1864, and I was four years old; the next year the War would end."

And that was how Belsnickel came at Christmas Eve.

* * *

The Belsnickel is almost as old as the first heavy wave of German immigrants into Pennsylvania. Earliest reference to the custom of Belsnickling is in the York *Gazette* of December 23, 1823 which warned Belsnickel to "keep within the limits of the hall." On December 24, 1825, this advertisement appeared in the Philadelphia *United States Gazette:*

"Mr. Grigg, in Fourth street, has food for the mind of the young, as well as the old, at his usual low prices so that when 'the stocking is hung up,' as of course it will be in all well regulated families, it is more probable that the bellsnickel will fill it in part, with more lasting sweets than those which the confectioner serves out—the latter, however, should by no means be omitted."

The Pottstown *LaFayette Aurora* of December 21, 1826, said:

"Bellsnickel. This is a mischievous hobgoblin that makes his presence known to the people once a year by his cunning tricks of fairyism. Christmas is the time for his sporting revelry, and he then gives full scope to his permitted privileges in every shape that his roving imagination can suggest. . . . . He has the appearance of a man of 50, and is about four feet high, red round face, curly black hair, with a long beard hanging perpendicular from his chin, and his upper lip finely graced with a pair of horned mustachios, of which a Turk would be proud; he is remarkably thick, being made in a puncheon style and is constantly laughing, which occasions his chunky frame to be in a perpetual shake; he carries a great budget on his back, filled with all the dainties common to the season—he cracks his nuts amongst the people as well as his jokes without their perceiving him. His antique clothing cannot pass unnoticed, as a description of its comical fashion may excite some ambition amongst the dandies, who are always on the lookout for something flashy and neat, beyond what an industrious, plain mechanic wears, to correspond their mode of dress to his, whose costume is entirely novel to the present generation; besides the French and English fashions are completely exhausted and have become obsolete; therefore a description of his grotesque raiment I presume will be acceptable.

"His cap, a queer one indeed, is made out of a black bearskin, fringed round or rather stuck round with porcupine quills painted a fiery red and having two folds at each side, with which he at pleasure covers his neck and a part of his funny face, giving sufficient scope for his keen eye to penetrate on both sides. . . . His outer garment, like Joseph's of old, is of many colors, made in the Adamitish mode, hanging straight down from his shoulders to his heels, with a tightening belt attached to the waist—the buttons seem to be manufactured entirely in the ancient style—out of the shells of hickory nuts, with an eye of whalebone ingeniously fixed in each,—when he runs, the tail of his long coat flies out behind, which gives an opportunity to behold his little short red plush breeches, with brass kneebuckles attached to their extremities, the size of a full moon. His stockings are composed of green buckram, finely polished. His moccasins are the same as those worn by the Chippewa nation. He carries a bow with a sheaf of arrows thrown across his miscellaneous budget, thus equipt he sallies forth in the dark of night, with a few tinkling bells attached to his bearskin cap and the tail of his long coat, and makes as much noise as mischief throughout our town, while the peaceable inhabitants are quietly reposing under the influence of Morpheus."

From the Philadelphia *Pennsylvania Gazette* of December 29, 1827:

"This Mr. Bellschniggle is a visable personage—Ebony in appearance, but Topaz in spirit. He is the precursor of the jolly old elf "Christkindle" or "St. Nicholas" and makes his personal appearance, dressed in skins or old clothes, his face black, a bell, a whip and a pocket full of cakes or nuts; and either the cakes or the whip are bestowed upon those around, as may seem meet to his sable majesty. It is no sooner dark than the Bellschniggle's bell is heard flitting from house to house, accompanied by the screams and the laughter of those to whom he is paying his respects. . . . .

Christkindle or St. Nicholas, is never seen. He slips down the chimney and deposits his presents in the prepared stocking."

The description of Bellsnickel as having a puncheon-like middle which is in a perpetual shake, is reminiscent of the poem by Clement Moore, "A Visit from St. Nicholas," in which the jolly elf is described as having a "round little belly that shook like a bowlful of jelly." In Moore's poem, however, his St. Nicholas is the benevolent one, who brings presents rather than punishment for past sins.

Belsnickel is found not only in the folklore of Pennsylvania, but the actual Belsnickel could be found wandering the towns on Christmas Eve in backwoods North Carolina, Virginia, and in Nova Scotia until the late 1920's.

The rural Belsnickel had his counterpart in the cities of the day. The urban Belsnickel was more in the nature of our Halloween trick-or-treat hobgoblin. In the Berks County Historical Society Library is the unpublished diary of James L. Morris, of Morgantown. Of the Belsnickel he says: "Dec. 24, 1831: Christmas Eve, saw two krisskintles tonight—the first I have seen in these many years. They were horrid, frightful looking objects." And, dating "Dec. 24, 1842: Christmas Eve—a few belsnickels . . . prowling about this evening frightening the women and children with their uncouth appearance—made of cast-off garments made particolored with patches, a false face, a shaggy head of tow, or rather wig, falling profusely over the shoulders and finished out by a most patriarchal beard of whatsoever foreign materials that could possibly be pressed into service."

From the Reading, Berks, and Schuylkill *Journal*, Dec. 27, 1851: "Parents, within doors, were making all sorts of purchases for distribution on the morrow—while juvenile harlequins were running from house to house, scattering nuts, confections, consternation and amusement in their way."

From the Easton *Daily Express,* Dec. 26, 1866: "Men and boys dressed in most fantastic garbs paraded the streets in numbers and caused considerable merriment to those who were fortunate enough to witness their amusing costumes and fantastic tricks."

From the Norristown *Herald and Free Press,* Dec. 31, 1851: "Christmas Eve was celebrated with processions of 'Kriss Kringles' arrayed in all their fantastic costumes, who paid their annual visit to the shopkeepers and citizens, soliciting the 'good things' and rendering an equivalent in caricaturing the sable sons of our soil."

The author is deeply indebted to the Pennsylvania Folklife Society of Kutztown, Pa., for the additional historical information of the Belsnickel.

My Grandpa's Beard

My grandpa's beard was snow-white and silky-soft. He looked like General Grant, I thought, but my grandma said he didn't. She said he ought to shave off his beard, that they weren't in style any more. But I told him he shouldn't, and he said: "Well, William, as you are one of the men of this family, I shall abide by your decision. I won't shave it off until you tell me to." And I never did tell him.

We had a lot of dead people in our house when I was little. My father said we had too many funerals . . . why don't we have a wedding once in a while. We did have a wedding once. It was down in Germantown outside of Philadelphia. It was my Cousin Charlie's wedding. His wife after he was married was my Cousin Hattie, the most beautiful woman in the whole world. We went to the wedding by train. We got there in the afternoon and had supper at my Uncle George's house. That was a funny house. There were only women, except my Uncle George. There was my Aunt Sue and their daughters—my cousins—Nina, Edna, Irma, Sue, and Madelaine. When it got late my Cousin Irma said she knew the way to Germantown and would take us. But she got lost, and we all got lost with her. But we did get to the wedding in time to eat some cake and ice cream. They had just about given us up, and we missed the preacher. But the ice cream and cake were good.

That was the only wedding we had for a long, long time. Always funerals. My Aunt Kate was the only one who had real fun at funerals. I mean she could always find something to laugh about at funerals. Aunt Kate was always laughing. She went to all the funerals, especially since there were lots and lots of "family."

She arrived at our house with Uncle Charles. My cousin Charles was named after him. Father loved to have Aunt Kate come to our house. My mother said she laughed too much, and one shouldn't laugh at the dead. But father said that the dead couldn't laugh at themselves, so we had to laugh for them.

Anyway, Aunt Kate used to tell some pretty funny stories.

Once, she said, there was a big funeral down country. All the family drove down. When they got there Aunt Lucy, had no mourning veil to wear. Thereupon my Aunt Kate said: "Lucy, you have to wear a veil. And you have to wear a big veil. Why Cousin John (he was the one being buried) is your own first cousin once removed on your own mother's side."

They looked all around and couldn't find a veil, until someone found a heavy black wool winter shawl. They put it over Aunt Lucy's head and poked eyeholes in it so she could see where she was going. It was a hot July day, and by the time Aunt Lucy got to the cemetery, she fainted from the heat. Aunt Kate said she scolded her because she didn't have the decency to wait until the funeral was over to faint. It wasn't THAT hot even with the wool veil.

At another time, my Aunt Kate attended a funeral in town where there was a parrot. Right when the preacher was saying: "I am the Resurrection and the Life," the parrot announced: "Time to get up!" Someone hurriedly threw a blanket over the cage, and the parrot said: "Time . . . awk . . awk." By the time they took off the blanket, he was almost smothered.

And another time, Aunt Kate recalled, one of the mourners from out of town had hired a rig to drive to the funeral. Everyone knows that livery stable horses always know where all the saloons are. This funeral was way out at the end of town, and every time the horse came to a saloon he pulled in to the curb, and the man driving had to yell: "Gee, you gol-durned drunken hoss!" and pull on the reins to yank him back into the funeral procession. My Aunt Kate laughed and laughed when she told those stories. Father laughed too, but mother commented, after Aunt Kate had gone home, "Kate ought to be ashamed of herself. Even death isn't sacred to her." Father said; "Kate will laugh at her own funeral," . . . and maybe she did.

I saw a Welsh funeral one time—an old-fashioned Welsh funeral. My grandpa always made fun of my grandma because she had Welsh blood. I never saw this kind of blood. I think it wasn't red like other blood but sort of blue.

My grandpa said my grandma must have been a queen one time. Maybe that gave her royal purple blood as I read of in my knighthood books. But he used to make fun of her because she could speak Welsh. He used to say to me: "That is a fool language, William. Do you know how that language first got spoken? Well, you know about the Tower of Babel, where they gave out the languages for all over the world?" And I said I did, that I learned that in Sunday School. And my grandpa said: "Well, when the Welshman was standing there to get his gift of tongues, he was looking right up in the sky with his mouth open and a pigeon. . . ." And my grandma said: "Will Harris, you shut up. Don't tell such nasty things to your own grandson!" But grandpa winked at me, and I knew just what that pigeon did.

Well, anyway, at this Welsh funeral everybody walked. They didn't have a hearse, with plumes on the horses and glass sides so you could see the coffin. They had sixteen men walk with the coffin. Eight at a time bore the coffin on their shoulders. They kept in step and walked until they were tired; then the other eight would step in and take the coffin. Each one of them wore a tall black hat with a big black crepe band with long streamers. In each crepe band was tucked a sprig of something green. I asked my mother what it was. She said: "Rosemary—that's for remembrance." When they were at the cemetery and the coffin was going down into the grave they all walked past the open grave and dropped their sprigs of rosemary on the coffin. And the people cried.

I was deeply sorry when my Uncle Bert died, as he was my favorite uncle. He wasn't married. He lived with my grandpa and grandma in Brooklyn. We went down there every summer, my mother, Aunt Eily, Cousin Doris, and I. Uncle Bert used to take me to Coney Island where we rode the chute-the-chutes, the steeplechase, roller coasters, and the loop-the-loop. I was the only one in Minersville who had ever looped the looped.

When Uncle Bert took sick and died, my father went down to Brooklyn for his body, which was placed in a box in the baggage car. He had to pay a carfare for him even if he was dead. I don't know what Uncle Bert died of, but after the funeral my father said: "Never again will we have so much as beer in this house." I was sorry my Uncle died of whatever it was, because I used to be sent to the "Eye-talian's" with ten cents to get a pail of beer on a summer night, and my father always gave me a penny, and the Eye-talian always gave me a bag of salty beer pretzels.

I liked funerals because there always was lots of good things to eat. If we went down country to a funeral for one of the freundschaff—family—there was always a lot more food then at funerals in town. That was because people had to drive long distances with a horse and buggy to get to the farm. They would have to start before daylight, I guess. After the funeral they would need lots of food so they could get back home without fainting from hunger.

Best of all were the pies and the cakes that people always brought to the family. I like the "funeral" pie best of all, although most people didn't. It was raisin pie and real juicy. There was always lots of it because people ate the other pies first. There was always boiled ham and maybe roast beef. There would be baloney and liver sausage and summer saus-age set off with plenty of pickles and hardboiled eggs and bread and butter. There would be big pots of coffee and pitchers of milk, schmierkäse and apple butter and potato salad and cole slaw and pepper cabbage. Even in our house where we weren't expected to provide a store of things to eat because there weren't many mourners from down country, we had lots to eat at funerals. I liked that.

I never laughed at my Aunt Kate's funeral jokes after I was ten years old.

That was the year of my saddest and most awful Christmas.

I had studied my *American Boy* and *Youth's Companion* advertisements and had written my Santa Claus letter. Of course I was too old to believe in Santa—but I wrote a letter "just in case." I don't remember what I asked for, probably some C. A. Stevens books, or G. A. Henty's or Horatio Alger's. Perhaps for some new skates, the key kind, for they had found their way into the coal regions a year before.

The Christmas tree had been sought, cut, and was standing in a pail of water on our back porch. I knew now that father and mother trimmed the tree with all the glittering ornaments that summered in a big old-fashioned painted tin tea box in the garret. But it still would be a heavenly surprise this year to see the tree illuminated for the first time by electric lights. Oh, yes, electric tree lights had finally arrived in our town, and we were to be one of the first families to use them. We had a whole string of seven lights—with carbon filaments. My father liked the real candles best, but the year before had put an end to them.

That was a hectic Christmas morning, if there ever was one. Father had the candles lighted, the room smelled happily of hemlock needles, the ornaments were in their proper places on the tree, with the tinsel angel on top. Trouble was, my cat Fritz was what Pennsy Dutch call "Wunnerfitzig". That is, he had a large bump of curiosity embedded under his thick maltese fur. When my dog Gyp scampered in from his bed behind the kitchen stove, Fritz was close on his tail. But while Gyp stopped to admire, Fritz kept on going right up the tree. A candle got knocked off its weighted perch. Flames licked a nearby branch. My father yelled: "Fannie! Get some water, the tree's afire!" He grabbed smouldering Fritz from the burning branch and threw him out the side door. I stood there howling. Gyp joined me. Father grabbed the bucket from mother and sloshed. His aim was good— and not so good. He put the fire out, but did so much damage to the wallpaper that we had to have Mr. Auchenbach come in to do it over again. We bought the electric lights.

But that was when I was nine.

Now I was ten, and it was Christmas time once more.

Two days before Christmas a big crate arrived for me from Brooklyn, New York. That was where my grandpa and grandma lived. Mr. Johnny Corcoran, the express man, brought it to our house and pointed out MY name on the shipping tag. That was the first time I ever got an express package sent to me.

As we never opened Christmas gifts until Christmas morning, the crate was stored away.

Now it was Christmas Eve.

When I came in from outdoors, the house was strangely silent. My mother was dabbing her eyes, and father looked very sad. They told me that my grandpa Harris was dead and that the undertaking men were going to bring his body to our house for the funeral. There would be no Christmas tree, no Christmas celebration this year.

I didn't care. I felt terrible. My grandpa was the nicest man in the whole world. He couldn't be dead! But he was.

The coffin was placed between the two front windows in our parlor. The lid was shut on the piano. I didn't have to practice while he lay dead there. The shades were drawn down and the shutters closed. They kept one of our electric lights on, the one that had a pink shade on it. But it was dark and scary. There were lots of flowers around, even though it was winter. They came from the florist, some all the way from Brooklyn with the coffin. They had a sickly-sweet smell. I didn't like it. I couldn't eat.

The funeral was two days after Christmas. All that time my grandpa lay there, and people went in to look at him. On the day of the funeral all of us in the family sat upstairs in the bedrooms and the hall while all the other relatives, cousins and such, and the friends and neighbors of the deceased sat downstairs. The preacher stood in the hallway at the foot of the stairs. He was the preacher they called "Old Gravy and Butter". I don't know what his name was—he was a Methodist like my grandma.

This preacher was always saying "One foot in the grave . . ah . . and the other all but . . . ah." I don't know what he said because all I could think about was how nice my grandpa was.

When the preacher stopped talking the people downstairs went out. Then we walked down the front stairs, and Mr. Weiser the undertaker was standing there with a big screw-driver ready to screw down the lid on the coffin. My mother took me and held me up and she held me right over my grandpa. And I looked at him. It was sort of like he was sleeping there. His snow-white beard was all combed out and it looked as silky soft as it always had.

Then my mother held me closer to my grandpa, and I could smell sort of a bad smell. She said: "Kiss Grandpa goodby!"

And she put my head down so my lips touched his beard, but the hair wasn't silky-soft any more. It was harsh and rough and sort of like straw. I started to holler and squirmed right out of my mother's grip. I ran out into the yard and threw up.

After the funeral I was allowed to open the crate my

grandpa had sent. I had to open it in my bedroom since that was where my presents were put during the funeral.

My father helped me open the crate with a hammer and screwdriver.

Inside was a big box wrapped in heavy store paper.

I took the box out and unwrapped it. There was the most beautiful tool chest in the whole world. My grandpa had made it all by himself. It was of solid oak with iron handles at each end. There was a lock, and the key was fastened to the chest top with gummed paper. When I unlocked the chest there was a tray in the top that was for nails and screws and small tools, like the screwdriver, carpenter's rule, pencil and pincers that were in it now. When you took the tray out, there was a place underneath for your tools. There was a handsaw, a keyhole saw, a hammer, a plane, a mallet, a chisel, a level, a square, and a brace and some bits.

I started to cry.

My father patted me on the back. I think he was crying too.

"Look," he said, "There's a letter for you."

I opened it.

It said: "To Build Your Dreams."

I didn't quite know what my grandpa meant—then.

"I Am the Last"

She stands there thin, stooped, a worn grey wool shawl pulled tightly across her shrunken breasts, her hands blue-veined, gnarled. Her eyes are grey, and the look in them is as of something far away. She is ninety-seven years old.

We are on the side porch of that place I once called home. Here I found my Flexible Flyer the Christmas Santa Claus brought me Gyp. There is where the ice cream freezer stood, swathed in an old carpet, waiting our return from the Fourth of July parade. There is the back yard where were my pigeons, my rabbits, my guinea pigs. There is where we built our clubhouse.

She speaks, slowly, softly. I have to listen carefully.

"Your father was a good man," she says. "He was a good man, a man everyone loved and respected. He was refined." That was her ultimate tribute, that word "refined." "I never was as good to him as I should have been. Oh, I kept his house clean. I cooked the things he liked. I loved him in my own way. But . . ." her voice trailed off.

"I never thought that I would live without him almost as long as I lived with him. I am thankful for the years I spent with him, but the years without . . ." again her voice crept into a sigh.

"It is a frightening thing, William," she whispered. "I am the last . . . No, don't say what you're going to say. I know I have you, and I know you love me. But it is a very frightening thing to me. I am the last. They are all gone. Until you are as old as I am, you will never realize what it means. They are gone. My father, my mother, my husband. All my brothers. My sister. All your father's kin. All my old friends.

Everyone I went to school with. Everyone I grew up with. My neighbors. They're all gone. I am the last."

She stood silent and, as I put my arm around her, I could feel her trembling.

She looked to the hills. Atop Pioneer Hill the cruel yellow gash of the strip mine power shovels showed where the great pines had been toppled in the last search for coal. On Lytle Hill there were no more trees. No more mountain laurel bushes. Only the spoil of the great shovels.

I knew that, if she were able to walk there, she would find none of the old stores left "over town." She would meet no friends, would deal with no old time storekeepers. No longer was there a Gyp to wait for a bone from the butcher. No butcher, no baker, no farmer stopped at her door. There was only the hateful, impersonal supermarket in which to fill her basket. There was no trolley to the county seat. There were no trains to Wanamakers. In Brooklyn, black faces peered from 1164 Fulton Street. There were no deep-throated colliery whistles to wake her up of a frosty morning. There were no trains waiting to take miners to work. The mines were shut down, every one of them.

The Grand Army was forgotten. Decoration Day was annually desecrated.

She still lived. She was ninety-seven. Her town was gone.

And she stood there, silent for a long time, and then she whispered: "I am the last."